Paying the Bill for International Education:
Programs, Purposes, and Possibilities at the Millennium

Alice Chandler

Published by NAFSA: Association of International Educators, 1307 New York Avenue, N.W., Eighth Floor, Washington, D.C. 20005-4701; www.nafsa.org.

Sponsored by the TOEFL Policy Council, test sponsor of the TOEFL Program at Educational Testing Service (ETS), Princeton, New Jersey.

ISBN 0-912207-82-5

ACKNOWLEDGMENTS

This study has been made possible through a generous grant from the International Perspectives Committee of the TOEFL Policy Council. I am grateful to the Committee for its financial support and also for its ongoing interest in and encouragement of this project. I should also like to extend my thanks to Julia To Dutka, Executive Director, Test of English as a Second Language (TOEFL), at the Educational Testing Service.

The questions posed and answered in "Paying the Bill for International Education" originated with the NAFSA Association of International Educators, which has maintained overview throughout this yearlong project. I am grateful to NAFSA for posing a challenging and important question and also for its willingness to accept the evolution of the study from a review of funding sources to a broader examination of the connections between funding, programs, partners, and policies. My especial thanks to Gail Hochhauser, Senior Directors of Special Programs at NAFSA, who has been an invaluable and unflagging resource person for me.

The breadth of the review of the current status of international education has required me to consult with experts in many fields. During the writing of this book, interviews were conducted with many professionals. For their participation, thanks are due to the following individuals: Mary Ashley, division chief, advising, teaching, and specialized programs, USIA; Peter Becskehazy, chief of advising branch, USIA; Joan Claffey, executive director, Association Liaison Office, American Association of State Colleges and Universities (AASCU); Richard Ekman, secretary, Mellon Foundation; Madeleine Green, vice president for research, American Council on Education; Virginia M. Hammell, CPA, Office of Inspector General, USDA; Paul Hiemstra, chief of specialized programs branch, USIA; and Ralph Hines, director, international education and graduate programs, Department of Education.

Thanks also go to: Joseph Johnson, vice president of education & global initiatives, Association of Colleges and

Universities (AAC&U); Hiram Larew, director, international programs, USDA Cooperative State Research, Education and Extension Service; Michael McCarry, executive director, Alliance for International Educational and Cultural Exchange; Joyce Scott, former vice president for academic programs, AASCU; Helen Seidler, director of international programs, American Association of Community Colleges (AACC); Jane Spalding, director of programs, AAC&U; Toby A. Volkman, program officer, education, knowledge and religion, Ford Foundation; and Emily Vargas-Baron, deputy assistant administrator, USAID.

Alice Chandler
President Emerita
State University of New York at New Paltz

ADVISORY BOARD

M any thanks are due to the following individuals who served as members of the Advisory Board: Dolores E. Cross, President, Morris Brown College; Robert A. DeVries, Former Program Director; W.K. Kellogg Foundation; Alice Ilchman, Chairman of the Board, The Rockefeller Foundation; Richard D. Lambert, Professor Emeritus, University of Pennsylvania; Jules LaPidus, President, Council of Graduate Schools; C. Peter Magrath, President, NASULGC; Patti McGill Peterson, director, Council for International Exchange of Scholars (CIES); Cassandra Pyle, Chair, Board of Directors, AED; Wendell G. Rayburn, Sr., Vice President for Administration and Finance, AASCU; Loren Renz, Vice President for Research, Foundation Center; Piedad F. Robertson, Superintendent/President, Santa Monica College; and Humphrey Tonkin, President Emeritus, University of Hartford.

PREFACE

Soon we face the advent of a new millennium. There is anticipation and trepidation about the next thousand years and what they will mean for inhabitants of this nation and our world. As we look to the future, we are mindful of what has transpired during the present millennium—events that have affected our lives and those of prior generations. It is overwhelming to think about inventions and discoveries that made it possible for people to live more productively during the past 100 years. It is equally overwhelming to observe that the urge to see "the world yonder" is still as strong as ever despite the apparent perceptual shrinkage in space and distance between and among continents. In our most recent history, we have entered cyberspace, where we communicate via e-mail, voice mail, and through other high technology innovations. Global economic forces have enabled 200 million people in India to become members of the middle class and entrepreneurs in the Silicon Valley to become millionaires on a daily basis. Yet, while some segments of society experience prosperity, there are still many economic, cultural, and social issues that need resolution for others to reach their full potential. At the core of this paradigm is the human spirit, aspiring to attain a better quality of life through access to education and to opportunities.

During the past 50 years, Educational Testing Service (ETS) has demonstrated a commitment to enabling international students to gain access to educational opportunities. The Test of English as a Foreign Language (TOEFL), which has been administered since 1964, has assisted colleges and universities in identifying qualified international students. For 35 years, the TOEFL test has remained a leader of and a standard for English language proficiency assessment throughout the world. In 1998, the TOEFL program introduced its first computer-based test. With the implementation of this new technology, ETS is proud to continue its tradition to serve colleagues, families, and students with assessment products of exceptional quality.

TOEFL is honored to partner with NAFSA on this important project of reviewing the changing context for international education in the United States. Through her insightful analysis, Alice Chandler has challenged the profession to reflect upon its responsibility to wrestle with the rapid changes shaping the landscape of international education. The shifts in the locus of activities can be dramatic, but the responsibility to guide the development of international education is integral to the mission to educate students. Recognizing that learning and teaching form the foundation upon which higher education is conceptualized, disciplinary knowledge, curricular innovations, and pedagogical ingenuity need to serve as catalysts to effect substantive and organic transformation in the conception and practices of international education.

As we embark on this journey of re-envisioning international education, I look forward to continuing collaboration with NAFSA and our old and new partners worldwide.

Julia To Dutka
    Executive Director
    Test of English as a Foreign Language (TOEFL)
    Educational Testing Service

FOREWORD

NAFSA is pleased to be a partner in producing this study detailing the trends in international higher education in the United States. As the front line of international student exchange on college and university campuses, NAFSA members grasp the impact of the changing trends in the focus and funding of international education initiatives.

Successfully preparing young people for the demands and responsibilities of a global economy requires foreign language study, interdisciplinary and intercultural study, and immersion in other cultures. Yet achieving greater emphasis on international education, from academic, campus-based programs to study abroad and foreign student participation on U.S. campuses, requires commitment and strategies beyond that which currently exists.

This paper is an important step in understanding what is required. Dr. Chandler has defined the framework, documented the trends, identified examples to motivate others to explore new possibilities, and issued challenges to the universities and colleges, the public sector and the corporate sector, as well as the foundation community, that reinforce the interdependency of the solutions to these problems.

I encourage your thoughtful review and consideration of these findings, as well as your active contribution to the action steps required.

Marlene M. Johnson
Executive Director and CEO
NAFSA

CHAPTER ONE

THE CHANGING CONTEXT OF INTERNATIONAL EDUCATION

We are all internationalists today. Consciously or not, Americans are immersed in the vast flows of international travel, communication, commerce, and interdependency that characterize global society at the turn of the millennium. In this new world order, airline passengers leap continents in hours; information and ideas circle the earth electronically in less than half a second; and $1.3 trillion dollars move daily through international currency exchanges[1]. The network of international relationships grows constantly more complex and intertwined.

Events since the end of the Cold War have accelerated both global prosperity and global interlock. The Gross World Product has grown by more than 40 percent since 1980, with the upswing accelerating in recent years (Mazur and Sechler 1997, 13). Centralized, hierarchical, and undemocratic political structures have given way to more decentralized and democratic forms of government in many areas of the world, and the resultant openness of society has quickened the flow of resources and ideas and accelerated the growth of trade.

The expanding worldwide economy has been particularly important to American economic well-being. International trade, tourism, and investments generate more than 15 million jobs domestically, and 5 million Americans are employed by foreign-owned businesses operating in the United States. Between 1990 and 1995, exports generated more than one-third of America's economic growth (ACE 1998, 1, 3).

Trade with developing countries has been an increasingly significant portion of the world's economic flow. During the 1990s, U.S. trade with developing countries has been expanding at twice the rate of export growth to the industrialized nations and now accounts for 35 percent of all export purchases (USAID 1998, 5; Carnegie 1992, 83).

But the globalization of commerce, people, and ideas has also created problems of unprecedented magnitude and complexity. The widening gap between global "haves" and "have nots" means that the least-developed countries are not participating in rising global prosperity. The poorest countries, with 42 percent of the world's population, receive only 6 percent of all private investment, even though many of their inhabitants live on the "knife-edge of survival" (Mazur and Sechler 1997, 16). Without basic sanitation, nutrition, and health care, billions of poor people in poor countries endure living conditions that contrast starkly both with the lives of the more affluent within their own countries and with the dramatic worldwide rise in health, life expectancy, and social conditions.

The widening gap between rich and poor and the soaring number of people living in poverty endanger world stability. Poverty and the dramatically unequal distribution of wealth and resources accentuate pre-existing tribal, ethnic, and intranational conflicts that in turn lead to the mass movement of refugees and immigrants across borders and sometimes across continents. Health problems and diseases also jump continents and will increasingly do so as the global flow of goods and peoples continues to rise. The urgency of these problems in many cases distorts our perception of the total reality of poorer nations—the richness of their art and culture and their resourcefulness in coping with difficult living conditions.

Global connectedness is especially evident in regard to the environment. Profligate use of resources by the industrialized nations and the untrammeled exploitation of natural resources in developing nations contribute to climate change, species loss, soil erosion, and water shortages. These problems, too, come home to the United States, as when forest fires in Mexico darken the skies of the American Southwest.

THE IMPORTANCE OF INTERNATIONAL EDUCATION

International education—which comprises internationally-related study, academic exchanges, and research—is critical to the development of intelligent world citizenship. Both altruism and self-interest demand "global stewardship"—a recognition of the interconnectedness of nations, of the need to narrow the gap between "have" and "have not" nations, and of the worldwide obligation to address global problems of health, population, and environment. Foreign trade and foreign policy are no longer elitist domains. They are the necessary and proper concerns of an informed citizenry and an integral requirement for America's educational system.

A globally intertwined economy also places heavy demands on international education as an instrument for economic development. Worldwide commerce in goods, services, and ideas is critical to continued American prosperity. But a worldwide economy demands a workforce that is aware of economic interdependency, knowledgeable about current affairs, receptive to differences in culture and tradition, and—ideally—fluent in at least one foreign language. Both in their jobs at home and in their contacts abroad, Americans increasingly deal with nations other than their own. The capacity to work constructively across cultures not only enriches their lives but gives them—and this country—a competitive edge in the scramble for leadership in the international marketplace. With the number of immigrants continuing to rise, international education also provides a valuable context for understanding cultural diversity at home as well as abroad.

Higher education is front and center in all aspects of international education—curriculum, exchange programs, and research activities. Elementary and secondary schools are important in developing a sense of global consciousness and providing an information base for further study. It is especially valuable to start foreign language training young. But it is up to the colleges and universities, whose programs build on that earlier knowledge and awareness, to:

- educate an informed electorate;
- provide professional training for a globalized economy;
- train foreign affairs specialists;
- sponsor educational and cultural exchange programs;
- conduct internationally-related research;
- manage development assistance programs; and
- assist in human-capacity building abroad.

BALANCE SHEET ON INTERNATIONAL EDUCATION

With such important international roles to play both at home and abroad, what is the status of international education in the United States? Are America's general education programs sufficient to the task of creating a globally knowledgeable citizenry? Are its professionals and specialists trained adequately and in adequate numbers? Are America's continuing education capabilities adequate to the needs of emerging nations, or are we failing to make appropriate use of the new communications technologies available to us? What lessons are to be drawn from the relatively slow growth of international student enrollments during much of this decade or from what appears to be the tendency to focus on short-term assistance and training activities rather than longer-term research and graduate education programs?

The answers, as this report will show, are mixed in regard to all these questions. International education curriculums are changing, largely in response to new communications technologies and the demands of foreign trade. But whether the pace or scale of change is adequate is another question. Enrollments in foreign languages, for example, are at an all-time low, and area studies and international relations both are having difficulties in coming to grips with needed multidisciplinary approaches. Thanks to distance-learning technologies, the number of overseas academic programs originating in American colleges and universities has proliferated in the past few years, but the quality and relevance of these programs remains untested. The commitment of these colleges and universities to international education for their own domestic students is also unclear.

Similar ambiguities surround the issue of exchange programs. International student enrollments in the United States are at an all-time high, but they grew very slowly for most of the decade. While faculty contacts abroad are multiplying electronically, they are declining physically. Shrinking dollars for graduate study abroad suggest that the pool of faculty with international experience will continue to fall in the future.

Overseas research projects give similarly mixed messages. American colleges and universities are still viewed as powerhouses of expertise. But much of the funding for research and development-assistance has shifted from long-term basic research programs to short-term applied projects. One of the most significant developments of recent years has been the emergence of nontraditional players, such as regional and community colleges, on the international scene and their involvement in short-term overseas training projects funded by business corporations. But these new programs do not support needed curricular development and do not address basic questions about the scope and objectives of international education on campus.

FUNDING FOR INTERNATIONAL EDUCATION

Funding is indissoluble from programs. Much of the uncertainty regarding international education is related directly to shifts and declines in traditional funding sources. Public colleges and universities have been hard hit for almost a generation by reductions in public support that have reduced their capacity to hire new faculty or launch new program initiatives. Many private institutions have experienced similar financial stringency. Federal funding remains a significant source of support for many international ventures; but budget cuts and policy changes for at least two major federal agencies—the Agency for International Development and the United States Information Agency—have significantly cut into their ability to support U.S.-based international research and training activities. Similar cuts in such long-time academic staples as the Fulbright Program have had comparable impact on exchange programs, although several new programs have been developed with the eastern European countries. The recent expansion of funding for Title VI programs is a bright spot in an otherwise discouraging picture.

Foundation funding, too, shows both positive and negative directions in regard to the funding of international education programs. Overall funding is up for international activities at academic institutions, but the focus of giving has shifted to applied and short-term training or assistance activities. In-country grants to local, non-governmental organizations are increasingly replacing support to U.S.-based colleges as part of a deliberate emphasis on grassroots, practical programs with clearly defined and seemingly doable outcomes. In some cases, the in-country program is linked to an American college or university, but such pairings appear to be rare.

In so financially stringent an environment for international education, business and corporate support for overseas training programs is increasingly important and is involving an expanded range of institutions, notably community colleges, in business-related international ventures. Such funding has the advantage of broadening the base of international involvement among higher education institutions in this country. But it cannot supply the fundamental need for faculty and facilities that colleges and universities are currently experiencing, nor is it geared to projects without a clear and immediate "bottom line."

OUTLOOK FOR INTERNATIONAL EDUCATION

The internationalization of society would seem to make the internationalization of higher education inevitable. But such tendencies as the decline in foreign language enrollments, the slow growth of international student enrollments, and the apparent shrinkage of internationally-related research activities make that conclusion questionable. Where the pressures are strong enough—as with business schools—curriculum appears to be changing significantly. But inertia is also a powerful factor. It is not clear that the majority of American college graduates are receiving the international education that they and society require or that we are building the intellectual capacity, through research and graduate study, to address some major world problems. The focus on short-term crisis intervention is understandable in a world dominated by emergency situations; but the role that can be played by American colleges and universities in basic research and long-term human capacity building needs to be reinforced. The words of the 1979 President's Commission on Foreign Languages and International Study still resonate today: "We are profoundly alarmed by what we have found: a serious deterioration in this country's language and research capacity, at a time when an increasingly hazardous international military, political, and economic environment is making unprecedented demands on America's resources, intellectual capacity, and public sensitivity."

A renewal of commitment to all dimensions of international education—general education, professional and specialized training, research and development assistance, human-capacity building, and student and scholar exchanges—is essential for America's future. The higher education community has a responsibility to make a far greater and more coherent commitment than it has done so far. But federal and state governments, as well as private foundations and the business community, must also look to their priorities. If there is one lesson to be learned from international education, it is the interdependency of our global environment. The quality of American life in the twenty-first century will largely depend on our ability to compete in an international economy and on our capacity and willingness to address global policy problems. How boldly we will embrace the purposes of international education and what combination of partners will pay the bill for international education remains to be seen.

---

1. *All dollar amounts are U.S. dollars.*

CHAPTER TWO

INTERNATIONAL EDUCATION RESPONDS TO CHANGE

Higher education has responded to global change in many ways. International education curriculums have expanded. Exchange programs have proliferated. International student enrollments have more than tripled in the past quarter-century. Research and development assistance programs have increasingly shifted to meet new needs, and the telecommunications revolution has multiplied the possibilities for international scholarly collaboration. Indeed, existing trends already foretell the increasing integration of business, technology, and education in the coming century, as new technologies dramatically alter classroom instruction and distance learning modalities globalize the reach of that instruction. The increasing number of international telecourses, the surge in academic-business partnerships, and the increasing reliance on colleges and universities to manage technical training abroad are all indicators of a growing worldwide "knowledge economy."

Viewed simply as an industry, higher education itself has become international. World trade in all forms of education currently totals $28 billion and is projected to reach $88 billion by the year 2025[1]. The United States Department of Commerce has estimated that international students contributed $8.3 billion to the American economy in 1997 (October 1998 Survey of Current Business.) and that education is among the nation's five largest export industries, including air travel, shipping, and tourism. The teaching of English as a second language is a $20 billion global service industry (Pesek 1997, 81–82).

By almost every measure, the internationalization of higher education appears to be growing in concert with the growing internationalization of the world. In the United States, the enrollment of international students is now at a peak. Enrollments at U.S. schools of international studies grew markedly during the first half of the 1990s—more than 70 percent at the undergraduate level and 40 percent in graduate studies (Goodman, King, and Ruther 1994, 17–19).

Colleges and universities also report a rising interest in study abroad on the part of American students.

For the most part the international education picture is an exciting and dynamic one. But there are missing elements as well. Like a photograph emerging from a developing bath—or an illustration filling itself in on a computer screen—international education has yet to emerge in full clarity or detail. Some of the constraints are intellectual— the unreadiness or unwillingness of campuses to place international education high on their priority list. But funding inadequacies are paramount. Recent cutbacks in state, federal, and foundation funding for many forms of international education seriously hamper needed growth in these areas. The business community is, to some degree, filling these gaps; but its role can only be a partial one. Achieving the level of internationalization of higher education needed in the twenty-first century will require the cooperation of all stakeholders. Colleges and universities must rethink the importance of international education and, if necessary, recast their academic priorities to assure their students of an education appropriate to the world they live in. But state and federal governments, private philanthropic organizations, and the business community all have imperative roles to play if international education in the United States is to meet the demands of a globalized century.

CHANGES IN CURRICULUM: POSITIVE DIRECTIONS

International education has been defined as "that body of activities which increases the knowledge of other countries or which engages Americans in contact with individuals and institutions outside the United States" (Building 1994, 1). Although it includes both research and exchanges, its most fundamental dimension is the curriculum. There can be no international education without a global dimension to the curriculum. Ideally, that curriculum will include all or most of the following disciplinary approaches:

- general education,
- area studies,
- international relations,

- foreign languages and cultures, and
- comparative and international approaches to individual subject areas.

International curriculums are also increasingly problem-oriented, approaching the contemporary world through such topics as environmental, global, and peace studies (Pickert 1992, 1). International education programs can be approached at different levels of specificity, from the education of generalists as part of the liberal arts curriculum to the training of internationally-oriented professionals and specialists in international affairs.

General Education

More than a decade ago, Ernest Boyer called for a core curriculum centered on international issues. He suggested that colleges could design global issues curriculums that focused on "essential questions of survival on earth," such as the environment or impact of population growth. Alternatively, campuses might establish curriculums that explored the basic questions of existence shared by all cultures (Monaghan, 1990, A30). Although many colleges and universities have taken international education as *a* theme or *the* theme of the core curriculum, little evidence exists for general adoption of such a focus, or even such an emphasis nationwide.

In some cases, multicultural programs that deal with the global origins of American diversity blur into international studies. But, global perspectives have yet to be adopted across the board. Interestingly, in many cases where such courses are mandated, they are seen as part of a skills component that groups international education with analytical and communicative proficiency. The assumption would appear to be that international perspectives are part of the intellectual "toolkit" that students need to carry into the twenty-first century. It is unclear whether the sense of global stewardship and common humanity to which Boyer referred is also part of such programs.

In 1990, Oregon State University adopted a bacca-
laureate core requirement that emphasizes critical think-
ing, diversity, and international issues . . . Both Missouri
Southern State College and Saint Michael's College are
weaving international themes throughout their courses
of study . . . Lewis and Clark Community College in
Illinois demands that all general education courses
devote attention to written and oral communication as
well as intercultural and international themes.
(Monaghan, A30).

Area Studies

Recent changes in academic programs and curriculums for
area studies clearly reflect the greater fluidity of global
society. The permeability of boundaries, the large-scale
international movements of goods and people, the ending of
old political orthodoxies, and the shift from bipolar to
multipolar international relationships have all challenged
the established fixity of geographic areas. The international
diaspora of scholars and scholarship has also contributed
to global change. Knowledge and ideas are no longer
containable within traditional boundaries, and even the most
closed of societies are penetrated and influenced by new
concepts and new information via the Internet. The fast-
moving global forces of the late 1990s, which frequently
focus world attention on relatively unknown regions, make
area studies and area expertise increasingly important to
world security. Such changes inevitably undermine the

With the help of a Ford Foundation grant, Duke
University is supplementing its traditional area studies
curriculum with a conceptual overlay that looks at the
impact of seas and shorelines on human interaction . . .
Also with Ford Foundation assistance, the University of
Texas, El Paso, has initiated an oral history project to
analyze the multigenerational experiences of Mexicans
on both sides of the border. (Volkman, 1998, 28–29).

existing curricular rigidities. The most dynamic area studies programs have responded to change by becoming more interdisciplinary and problem-oriented, looking at their subject matter topically as well as geographically.

International Relations

Like area studies, international relations (IR) is by definition interdisciplinary. It focuses on the political, economic, and cultural relations between sovereign states in a world without an overarching central authority. IR is usually viewed as divided into two clusters of study: one dealing with such areas as power politics and security studies, the other with international political economy (issues of trade, technology, investment, and finance). (Lebow 1996, B1.)

Tensions and dissent mark the intellectual substance of IR today. Indeed, the discipline has been described as "a political as well as an academic battleground" (Hill 1994, 13). The abrupt ending of the Cold War caught many IR theorists unprepared and challenged some of their basic theoretical assumptions about the nature of power. At the same time, emerging global economic issues and new topics, such as human rights and the environment, have tilted IR in different directions. Even the more traditional area of security studies is changing, as scholars come to realize that international political relationships cannot be studied without analysis of ethnic and cultural forces (Lebow 1996, B2.)

The discipline also seems preoccupied with many of the methodological issues characteristic of postmodernism and its rejection of objective truth as a possible outcome of study. Added to these methodological difficulties are the controversies surrounding the political role of international relations specialists and the degree to which they are or should be involved with foreign policy decisionmaking. More than any other internationally-related discipline, IR is in a state of flux.

Foreign Language and English as a Second Language (ESL)

Pedagogy in these areas is changing rapidly. Advances in learning technology have revolutionized the way in which languages can be taught. CD-ROMs, interactive audio and video, local and long-distance networks, and satellite broadcasts substitute interactive programming for endless drill. Aided by these technologies, students participate in real-life dramatizations of language use. They can tune into foreign television or radio, read foreign newspapers online, or even correspond internationally by e-mail. Both foreign language and ESL students benefit greatly from the instant playback feature of much language teaching software, which enables them to compare their pronunciation with that of the foreign speaker. The frontier is open for imaginative classroom change in all areas of language instruction.

Creighton University uses computers, fax machines, and satellite technology to transmit the front pages of major foreign language newspapers to U.S. campuses for their foreign language programs and language laboratories (Watkins 1991, A23). Students at Stanford University can use computers to create talking foreign language comic books that can help them master conversational nuances. (Wilson 1992, A24).

Business Programs

Not surprisingly, in view of the globalization of the economy, business schools are becoming leaders in foreign language and foreign culture instruction. The International Association for Management Education[2] now offers faculty seminars and workshops on globalizing the business curriculum. Universities such as Eastern Michigan, Clemson, Southern Illinois, and the University of Tennessee at Knoxville combine requirements in area studies and foreign language proficiency with their international business economics programs. These pioneering programs served as the models for the federal government's establishment in 1988 of the 16 Centers for International Business Education and Research (CIBERS) (Voght and Schaub 1992, 1,3). Such internationalized business curriculums are of special importance to the growing number of students interested in private sector jobs with an international dimension rather than in traditional foreign service positions.

> San Diego State University has collaborated with the
> Paris Chamber of Commerce and Industry to offer
> training in teaching commercial French and French
> business practices...The University of South Carolina
> and the University of Hawaii provide summer institutes
> that teach business faculty how to internationalize
> their curriculums through interdisciplinary studies.
> (Voght and Schaub 1992, 1,3).

Teacher Education

Progress is also being reported in internationalizing the
critical field of teacher education. Recognizing the importance
of internationalizing elementary and secondary school
curriculums, some states have developed global education
programs. Wisconsin, Minnesota, and California have
programs to assist in curriculum planning, promote staff
development, or identify model learner outcomes.

> Florida International University's Global Awareness
> Program offers international studies to pre-service and
> in-service schoolteachers . . . Ohio State University
> links student teachers with internationally minded
> classroom teachers. (Haakenson 1994, 1).

Other Disciplines

Fields, such as engineering, with strong international
orientations are also expanding globalization efforts within
the curriculum. Indeed, there appears to be a general
tendency at many institutions to intertwine international
studies with other disciplines, especially the cognate
disciplines of history, economics, and political science.

Libraries, Databases, and Distance Learning Technologies

Technology is also assisting in the international sharing of
libraries and databases. The global availability of knowledge
is a potent tool in equalizing the vast differences in
educational systems among nations, particularly in

Mary Baldwin College combines programs in foreign
language, anthropology, and ethnic studies into a
single department of foreign languages and cultures . . .
Oregon State University students are able to graduate
with two masters degrees: in their original major and in
international studies in the same discipline. To earn
the second degree students must take four years of a
foreign language and study abroad for at least 10
weeks. (Cage 1995, A16; Magner 1994, A19). (Since
1982 Oregon has been utilizing international students
to educate Americans by giving them the difference
between resident and nonresident tuition).

developing and newly industrialized countries, where tight
finances do not permit the acquisition of adequate library
resources. Widely and appropriately shared, and with the
necessary quality control mechanisms, these new
technologies give promise of helping to create what some
have termed the "worldwide electronic university." With
multimedia systems creating virtual realities and with
computer networking enabling scholars to deal with
problems of unprecedented complexity, the new millennium
thus offers unprecedented opportunities for international
educational cooperation. Fulfillment of these potentialities,
however, may be delayed by the slow technological growth in
many of the poorer nations.

The Online Mendelian Inheritance in Man database at
Johns Hopkins University is available free around the
world . . . Cornell University provides researchers
around the world with access to AGRICOLA, the
database of the National Agricultural Library, as well as
to BIOSIS, a major genetics database (Rossman 1992,
55, 68).

REQUIREMENTS FOR FURTHER CHANGE

According to Richard Lyman, President Emeritus of Stanford University, "American higher education has not yet responded adequately to an international environment that increasingly . . . tests our capacity to meet global challenges." Lyman acknowledges that American colleges and universities have, in recent years, increased their international course offerings, expanded their international library holdings, tended to hire more faculty with international expertise, and promoted greater opportunities for faculty and students to study abroad. But he also comments on our general "American ignorance of world geography, a lack of proficiency in foreign languages, and cultural parochialism when attempting to operate in an international setting" (Hanson and Meyerson 1995, xiv-xv).

The most dramatic evidence of weakness in the internationalization of higher education lies in the decline of college-level foreign language studies. The United States compares poorly with Japan and the western European nations, both in the foreign language expertise of its general population and in the available expertise in foreign languages and cultures. In any given semester, fewer than 10 percent of American college and university students are enrolled in a foreign language course, and more than half the students in that small group are studying Spanish. Between 1990 and 1995, enrollments in French and German fell by roughly 25 percent. In Russian they dropped almost 45 percent during that same period. For the year 1997–98, only 261 college and university tenure-track jobs were available in all foreign languages in the entire country (Cage 1996, A12; "Unemployment Rate" 1996, A15). The unemployment rate for doctoral recipients in foreign languages continued near an all-time high even though the federal government alone lists at least 34,000 jobs requiring foreign language competence and 86 percent of corporations reported a need for managers and employees with greater global awareness ("Educating" n.d.). Only the self-designated "International 50" group of private liberal arts colleges report increasing foreign language enrollments (Engerman, 1992, passim). These colleges are an anomaly, but an anomaly that proves that change is possible.

Critics of both area studies and international relations curriculums are also troubled by what they see as retrograde tendencies in their disciplines. IR, in particular, has been criticized for relying on "fashionable scholarly theories that have not been tested against the vast changes in the global political landscape over the past ten years" and for being more interested in turf preservation than curricular change. Alumni in the field are said to be calling for new courses on "the meaning of freedom, the transitions to market-oriented economies and social systems, and the impact of information technologies on the creation and use of knowledge." In the wake of dramatic global change, IR is being redefined "not just as the study of diplomacy or politics among nations, but also as the study of the ever-expanding web of commercial and cultural networks that enhance people's ability to exchange goods and information, to project influence and values" (Goodman 1996, A52).

Internationalizing the curriculum requires administrative, and particularly presidential, leadership; but responsibility for implementation rests firmly with the faculty. A recent study by the Carnegie Foundation for the Advancement of Teaching finds that the professoriate of 14 major industrialized countries supports the internationalization of the curriculum and welcomes greater internationalization of science and scholarship. But the American professoriate ranks relatively low on the scale. Only 45 percent of the American professoriate think that the curriculum should be further internationalized; and only a little more than half of them rank connections with scholars in other countries as highly important, in contrast to the opinion of more than 80 percent of the professoriate in most other countries (Altbach and Lewis 1997, 186).

To some degree, the faculty's restrained interest in international scholarly collaboration reflects the global predominance of U.S. science and knowledge generally. But it may also reflect a structural resistance to programs, such as international education, that cross departmental boundaries and perhaps some continuing parochialism within the professoriate itself. In the face of tumultuous global change, even the Association of Professional Schools of International Studies reports only limited interest in multidisciplinary, problem-oriented approaches to international education.

EDUCATIONAL EXCHANGE PROGRAMS: POSITIVE DIRECTIONS

Faculty and student cultural exchanges are important elements of an internationalized educational atmosphere. The almost half million students from abroad now constitute about 3.4 percent of all U.S. higher education enrollments and 10.4 percent of all graduate enrollments (Davis 1998, ix, 2). Roughly 100,000 American students study abroad each year (Davis 1998, ix)—essential preparation for young people who will live and work in a world that increasingly requires the capacity to think and function across cultures.

In addition to personal benefits, international student enrollments and study abroad programs confer institutional advantages. Classroom perspectives are enlarged when international students ask value questions rooted in their own cultural backgrounds or raise questions on such issues as "world politics, political order, regionalism, or the processes of creating and redistributing power." If the purpose of higher education is the development of intellectual breadth and depth, a significant international student presence can genuinely change the classroom and campus environment.

International student enrollments also serve pragmatic purposes. As previously noted, foreign students contribute $8.3 billion a year to the American economy. They also cost-effectively fill unused seats in the classroom, especially in many underenrolled graduate programs, where their presence is a financial necessity. Despite recurring complaints about language problems, international teaching and research assistants add both to our talent pool and to the diversity of America's scholarly community[3]. The United States has never developed a national policy in regard to international students; other countries, such as Great Britain, Germany, Australia, and Japan, have aggressively pursued their enrollment.

Foreign Students

Student mobility mirrors world mobility. In 1997–98, 481,280 international students, the largest number ever recorded, were enrolled in regionally accredited American colleges and universities. Representing approximately 225 different countries, 57.6 percent of those students came from Asia, 14.8 percent from Europe, and another 10.6 percent from Latin America. Roughly 5 percent each came from Africa, the Middle East, and North America—thus providing American students with a worldwide mix of classmates (Davis 1998, 11, 14–17). A little more than half of the international students were enrolled at doctoral and research universities, reflecting the large number of graduate students in the mix. But substantial proportions were also distributed at state colleges and universities, independent liberal arts colleges, and community colleges (Davis 1998, 45).

One hundred twenty-five U.S. public and private colleges and universities enroll 1,000 or more international students. New York University is tops, with 4,964 international students out of a total enrollment of 31,609. (Davis 1998, x, 48).

Study Abroad Programs

Although only a tiny fraction of American college students take the opportunity to study abroad, that number is rising, too. In the past 10 years, the number of U.S. students earning credit for study abroad has doubled to almost 100,000—roughly 0.6 percent of all college enrollees. Although the majority of these students continue to attend western European institutions, the past few years have seen greater diversity in their destinations, including China, Poland, Australia, and Ecuador (Davis 1998, 89, 92–93). Service learning programs that link study abroad with community service or business experience are also becoming more popular, as are previously nonexistent study abroad options for engineering students. It will continue to be important over the next decade to ensure an adequate participation of minority students in study abroad programs—and, indeed, in all aspects of international education.

Recent studies confirm that the best way to master a foreign language is to go to the country where it is spoken. Empirical evidence shows that the study abroad experience converts novices into "fluent" speakers of the language. ("Researchers" 1997, A45).

Exchange Scholars

Foreign scholars studying and teaching in the United States and American faculty abroad also constitute a rich source of potential internationalization. More than 65,000 foreign scholars were affiliated with U.S. institutions in 1997–98. Four in 10 of them came from Asia (Davis 1998, 127). This movement of scholars and students across boundaries is more and more being facilitated by institutional agreements and partnerships. These linkages may promote the movement of students, or they may involve the creation of joint-degree programs. Some of the programs, such as the 34-campus U.S.-European consortium to promote exchanges for engineering students, involve a sizable number of institutions and often receive outside funding support.

Despite these collaborative programs, the rising number of foreign scholars in this country contrasts with what most observers believe is at best a stagnant number of American scholars going overseas. Thanks to telecommunications technologies, "virtual" connections with foreign colleagues are rising rapidly. But the real immersion in a foreign culture that comes from living abroad appears to be waning, as high living costs, family commitments, negative promotion policies, and international uncertainties undermine what was once a more robust commitment to living and studying abroad.

Six liberal arts colleges have established exchange programs with Brazil, Indonesia, and Turkey, designed to encourage more American undergraduates to study in those countries . . . Boise State University has developed a collaborative M.B.A. program with the National Economics University in Hanoi . . . Christopher Newport University and Beijing Polytechnic University have agreed to conduct exchanges and collaborate on laser research . . . Appalachian State University has cooperative arrangements with seven countries in Asia, Latin America and Africa to conduct collaborative research and course development. ("Consortium" 1995, A67; "Boise State" 1995, A44).

REQUIREMENTS FOR FURTHER CHANGE

The number of international students in the United States reached an all-time high of 481,280 in 1997–98, after six years of decelerated growth. However, a substantial portion of the rebound occurred in two-year colleges, which continue to attract growing numbers of international undergraduates interested in low tuition—at least for their first two years of study. It should also be noted that the upswing predates the Asian financial crisis, whose full impact will not be seen until 1999–2000. International students are only 3.4 percent of all U.S. college and university enrollments, a significantly lower fraction than that of France, Germany, or Great Britain (Davis 1998, ix, 84 - 85).

Soaring tuitions and the rising value of the dollar have contributed to slowing the growth of international enrollments by making education in this country more costly at the same time that a number of the developing and newly industrialized countries have been expanding their own higher educational opportunities. Other nations, such as England, Australia, and Canada are—with government support—competitively promoting their foreign student programs and recruiting away potential enrollees.

Deliberately or not, American public policy in regard to international students is often counterproductive. Sharply higher tuition for non-resident students at many public colleges and universities (as well as steep tuitions at private institutions) is having a negative impact on enrollments, as are the new federal immigration policies that many international students view as inimical to their needs ("New Law" 1996, A45). Nor do American colleges and universities adequately exploit the value of their international student enrollments, either to enrich their instructional environment or to promote an international environment on campus. An interesting discussion of the value of international students in the classroom by Allan E. Goodman, president of the Institute of International Education and former dean of the School of Foreign Service at Georgetown University, cites ways in which dialogue between foreign and domestic students can help American students develop the capacity "to see issues from the perspective of their adversaries" (Goodman 1996, A52).

Similar criticisms can be made in regard to American study abroad students. Lack of financial support makes it difficult for many of them, especially minority and nontraditional students, to take advantage of such programs. They are neither adequately prepared to benefit from their foreign experiences when they study abroad nor well-integrated into the intellectual life of the campus upon their return (Hanson and Meyerson 1995, xiv-xv).

It is also unclear whether America's colleges and universities sufficiently encourage international experiences for their faculties. High costs and difficult family living conditions, notably in regard to their children's schooling, appear to be making it harder for faculty to choose to live and teach abroad. (These problems are especially acute for two-career families.) But campus promotion policies, which often view study abroad as unrelated to professional growth, are also discouraging. Sharp cutbacks in Fulbright funding have reduced the number of U.S. scholars studying abroad by almost a third over the past decade (National Humanities Center 1997, 11).

America needs college and university graduates well-versed in international subject matter and with a world view that is imbued with an understanding of other nations and other cultures. The presence of international students and scholars in this country helps create that leavening at the same time that having an American-educated leadership cadre abroad is beneficial to this nation's trade and foreign policy goals. All forms of educational exchanges—international students, study abroad programs, and faculty exchanges—are vital to maintaining a scholarly community at the forefront of inquiry and to promoting the concept of international social stewardship. U.S. progress in promoting and utilizing such exchanges is not currently adequate. In the long run, we should be trying to develop an ongoing and permanent symbiosis between American institutions and those in other countries, whereby we share faculty resources and integrate academic programs to produce greater student mobility among all institutions

RESEARCH AND DEVELOPMENT ASSISTANCE: POSITIVE DIRECTIONS

Funded in large measure by research awards from the federal government, the contributions that American research universities have made to world betterment have been staggering. The Green Revolution and the Oral Rehydration Solution, both mainly the product of American academic research, have saved tens of millions of children and adults in developing countries from starvation, malnutrition, and death and have contributed to longer lifespans and to greater international prosperity. Research-based innovations and the application of technology to such areas as medicine, public health, and engineering have produced dramatic results in such areas as plant breeding, irrigation, weather satellites, information technology, oral contraceptives, rural electrification, and pest control. Especially in agriculture, such contributions dramatically benefit countries with the lowest per capita income, where technology-based growth in farming capabilities generates high economic returns. Such advances also benefit the United States, since every dollar invested in agricultural research for developing countries generates $4.39 in additional imports those countries can afford to make (Pinstrup-Anderson, Lundberg, and Garrett 1995, 1).

American doctoral campuses have also traditionally served as important destinations for international students seeking advanced degrees. These students often become professional and political leaders in their own countries, expanding the knowledge base in their home country and strengthening its personal and intellectual bonds with the United States. Today more than 200,000 international students—most of them self-funded—are enrolled in American masters or doctoral programs, about half of them at the masters level (Davis 1998, 21, 68).

Historically, the land-grant and large research campuses have been the leaders in educating foreign graduate students and applying America's research and technological expertise to the needs of developing countries. Today they are joined by many state colleges and universities and community colleges, which are participating in the information revolution by offering training programs tailored to meet the specific human resource development needs of emerging countries. Both these "designer" programs and broader spectrum curricular offerings are increasingly being offered through distance learning mechanisms, including the Internet. Recent studies show that half the new jobs in industrialized countries already require a minimum of 17 years of formal education as well as access to continuing education (Carnegie Commission 1992, 78). In addition to their traditional roles in offering research and graduate education, American colleges and universities now also serve as critical resources in meeting these needs for human-capacity development.

Independent liberal arts colleges also have a role to play in development assistance activities. To a surprising degree, large numbers of them also use their research capabilities for development assistance. Roughly 15 to 20 percent of some 200 small independent colleges report sharing resources and expertise in medicine, public health, and environmental problems with developing nations.

Iowa State University faculty now conducts about 30 cooperative agricultural projects with the People's Republic of China...ISU is also working with the leading Ukrainian agricultural university to help modernize its curriculum . . . Jackson State University engages in collaborative research on microeconomic development and environmental protection with Jomo Kenyatta University in Kenya (College of Agriculture 1997, n.p.). The University of Idaho and Leyden University in the Netherlands are cooperating on joint archaeological research projects . . . Marshall University shares in a research consortium with two other American campuses and higher education institutions in Europe, Mexico, and Canada (AASCU 1998, passim).

REQUIREMENTS FOR FURTHER CHANGE

As we shall see, cutbacks in state, federal, and foundation funding are taking their toll on the ability of American research universities to support graduate study and to participate in internationally-oriented research. But difficulties also exist in finding scientists capable of and willing to deal with the problems of developing countries. The lack of firsthand experience in living abroad often inhibits scientists from developing research agendas suitable to the technology and infrastructure of the countries with which they work. The accomplishments of such bodies as the Agricultural Research Centers and the Tropical Diseases Program of the World Health Organization show how dramatic scientific progress can be. But at the very time that telecommunications is making it easier for scientists to work globally, there appears to be some erosion in their actual engagement abroad.

SUMMARY

Along every traditional dimension of international education, the balance is finely struck. Change, often dramatic, is to be seen in specific curriculums and in the pedagogic strategies that are now made possible by technology. But college and university curriculums are still not pervasively internationalized and, in the case of foreign language study, the direction is retrograde.

International student enrollments are at a record high, and study abroad programs are growing quite rapidly. But the enrollment of such students decelerated during most of this decade, and study abroad programs, while growing rapidly, are still minuscule and poorly integrated into campus life as a whole—a criticism that can also be made of the use of foreign students as an educational resource. International faculty contacts have grown, thanks to telecommunications, but foreign experiences are neither a faculty nor an institutional priority. While the research contributions of American colleges and universities remain strong, the lack of firsthand experience abroad often makes it difficult for researchers to adapt their work to the needs of developing nations. With only about 4 percent of the world's expenditure on research and development and a mere 14 percent of its scientists and engineers, developing countries urgently need the collaboration of technologically advanced countries such as the United States to help reduce the income and knowledge gaps between rich nations and poor (Carnegie Commission 1992, 43). Although the expanding participation of state and community colleges in human-capacity development provides a critical educational resource for emerging economies in the newly industrialized countries, this nation cannot afford to ignore the importance of research and graduate education in ensuring a more stable world.

---

1. *An American billion is 1,000 million.*

2. *Formerly the American Assembly of Collegiate Schools of Business; name changed in 1997.*

3. *The presence of international graduate students does not absolve institutions from the active recruitment and support of domestic minority students. A positive step by the federal government is reflected in the 1998 Title VI International Education Programs, which adds an institutional development and study abroad program to assist historically black colleges and universities, Hispanic-serving institutions, and tribally controlled campuses in strengthening their international affairs programs.*

CHAPTER THREE

SHRINKING FEDERAL AND STATE SUPPORT

Funding for international education, as for all other educational programs, comes primarily from campus operating budgets. For public colleges and universities, these budgets represent a combination of state tax dollars and student tuition and fees. For private institutions, the major sources of revenue are tuition and endowment funds. It is these dollars that pay for international academic programs; provide scholarships for exchange students; fund faculty research and teaching activities overseas; and sustain needed library, laboratory, and instructional technology resources.

In recent years, both private and public institutional budgets have come under considerable stress. Inflationary pressures combined with massive new expenses, such as campus computerization and regulatory compliance costs, have driven tuitions at private campuses out toward the limits of affordability and have reduced institutions' financial flexibility. Persistent cutbacks in state support for public institutions have also resulted in tuition increases and have sharply reduced the number of dollars available for international education programs. Because dollars are scarce, faculty appointments and replacements tend to be limited to what are perceived as core disciplines and high-demand areas of the curriculum. Even research and other special programmatic activities that have historically been supported by federal funds have become increasingly self-funded as the proportion of government support has dropped. With both core operating support and federal programmatic funding reduced, budgetary pressures fall particularly heavily on international education, which tends to have no specific departmental constituency.

The future, however, may be somewhat more promising than the recent past. Despite the long-term erosion of resources, the financial picture for most public and many private institutions has brightened in the past year or two, and the increasing number of private-public partnerships between higher education and the business community also promises greater support for international initiatives. Right now, however, whether we look at state, federal, or—as we shall see in a later chapter—foundation grantmaking, the financial support available for international education programs is very much in flux. Continued loss of funding for international initiatives could undermine both instruction and research.

STATE FUNDING: STATUS REPORT

State support for public higher education has been seesawing for most of the past two decades. Although higher education constituted almost 10 percent of state expenditures in the mid-1970s, that figure had shrunk to approximately 7 percent by the mid-1990s, overtaken by expenditures in health, welfare, and corrections. Even the relative prosperity of the late 1980s and the 1990s did not reverse that trend. Only recently have higher education budgets again started to rise in a number of states. But between 1987 and 1996, the ratio of higher education expenditures per student to state per capita revenues fell in every state but two.

Inflationary pressures also have taken their toll. There were only three years between 1980 and 1996 in which appropriations for public colleges and universities matched the increases in the Higher Education Price Index. Among the most visible impacts of these reductions has been the shift from full-time to part-time faculty and the transfer of resources into the most heavily enrolled sectors of the curriculum. Nationwide reductions in foreign language instruction dramatically illustrate the impact of these cuts.

Rising tuitions at public colleges and universities, as well as at private institutions, have also been damaging to international education. The cost of public college and university tuition, room, and board increased 33 percent (in 1996 dollars) between 1975 and 1995. The cost of tuition, room, and board at private institutions rose 87 percent during the period. Enrollment by freshmen with family incomes below the all-families median has been falling at both public and private institutions since the 1970s

(Chandler 1998, 19–37), and these rising tuition costs have also affected foreign student enrollments, as shown by their recent movement toward lower-cost community colleges. Pushed by the need to find new tuition revenues without upsetting taxpayers, a number of states have not only increased the tuition at public campuses but have expanded the non residential (out-of-state and overseas) differential. Very little public funding is available for the support of international students, and scholarship dollars at private institutions are understandably driven toward sustaining the increasing needs of domestic students rather than being channeled toward students from overseas. The slowed growth of international student enrollments in the United States after the early 1990s is partly the result of these tuition increases, especially when experienced in conjunction with the rising value of the dollar.

Internationally knowledgeable and active faculty and students are singular assets for states seeking to expand foreign trade opportunities. Full-fledged partnerships between the states and their public and private colleges and universities could include greater reliance on (and support for) international university programs such as Title VI Centers, Centers for Internationalization of Business Education and Research (CIBERS), International Trade Centers, and exchange programs, as well as industrial and agricultural extension programs and small-business development centers. Strengthening such programs would have the doubly valuable effect of helping to underpin more basic university activities such as foreign language instruction and student exchange programs. Indeed, it has been argued that states should include among the measures they use to assess their "export readiness" the percentage of students in foreign language classes, the number of foreign students enrolled in their state colleges and universities, the percentage of state students studying abroad, and the percentage of faculty teaching or studying overseas.

REQUIREMENTS FOR FURTHER CHANGE

The past two years have seen an upswing in state funding for public higher education, but far from enough as yet to repair a long period of cumulative underfunding. Improvements in base funding need to be continued if campuses are to have the flexibility to reallocate significant resources into international education programs. States can reinforce such prioritization by providing special funds to support international program expansion; but states must also recognize the need to underpin the bread-and-butter expenses of international education: faculty, facilities, laboratories, libraries, and instructional technology.

Campuses, too, need to take advantage of the improving financial climate to begin implementing active programs of curricular internationalization, using creative means wherever possible. Low-enrollment languages, for example, which are unsustainable on any single campus, can become viable if shared among several institutions, either through joint appointments of faculty or through networked telecommunications programs. Particularly in disciplines connected with international studies, such as history or economics, plans should be laid out to provide global coverage. Coordinated appointments with business, education, and engineering schools—all of which have been expanding the international emphasis within their curriculums—may offer untapped resources, as can relatively modest investments in faculty retraining or travel grants.

Tuition and scholarship policies can strongly reinforce both foreign student enrollments and study abroad programs. State governments need to review the impact of higher out-of-state and foreign student tuitions on their ability to recruit adequately and, at a minimum, refrain from future disproportionate tuition increases. States should also review existing tuition and scholarship policies in regard to study abroad and set specific goals for increasing those numbers.

State governments need to realize the links between their economic development goals of increasing export trade and attracting foreign industry and the presence of campuses with strong international orientation as a reservoir of expertise, a source of foreign contacts, and a catalyst for change.

FEDERAL FUNDING: STATUS REPORT

Foreign policy and foreign relationships are constitutionally the province of the federal government. In the interest of creating a more stable world, the federal government has assumed a responsibility for providing technical assistance to developing nations in order to facilitate their transition to democracy and free-market economic viability. These federal responsibilities create a logical nexus between national interests and the capacity of the higher education community for instruction and research. Federal programs help set a national agenda for international education, identify emerging international trends and needs, and leverage the private moneys that also support scholarships, exchanges, and other international initiatives.

Although government relationships with academia remain generally strong, a troubling recent trend has been the decline in federal funding for several of the key agencies and programs responsible for maintaining international educational activities. These funding cuts are part of a broader range of reductions in support for foreign affairs generally. But they fall with special weight on the higher education community, which historically has relied on the federal government to assume much of the supplemental cost of international research and education programs. Such international programs build upon the existing funding base of the university but extend these resources to serve both the international advancement of knowledge and the nation's foreign policy goals.

Prior to their recent consolidation, more than 35 federal agencies sponsored educational and cultural exchanges, and the number of programs is still daunting. This study will

focus on four leading federal agencies—the Agency for
International Development (USAID); the United States
Information Agency (USIA); the international education and
foreign language programs under the Department of
Education (DOE); and the National Security Education
Program (NSEP) of the Department of Defense (DOD). All of
these agencies have had and continue to have significant
interaction with colleges and universities, but funding
declines and changing priorities are rapidly altering the
shape and scope of that relationship.

United States Agency for International Development (USAID)

The mission of USAID is to promote sustainable development
in developing and transitional countries. Such assistance is
critical to America's role as a world leader and also to its
economic prosperity. By promoting social and economic
progress in these nations, USAID programs help to create a
greater demand for American goods and services and to
expand cooperative and stable relationships between this
country and the nations it assists.

Because developing nations lack the resources and technical
skills needed for modern society, much of the USAID
portfolio is research-oriented and includes both long-term
"strategic" research and short-term applied activities. Despite
the long payoff time, it is strategic research—especially in
health, population, and agriculture—that has had the most
profound impacts. As stated in the 1996 USAID Research
Report, the agency engages "U.S. universities and community
colleges as partners in many of our research efforts. Much of
the field and laboratory research that USAID supports
[around the globe] is conducted in U.S. institutions of higher
education" (11). Indeed, the collaboration between USAID
and the higher education community has been inseparable
from these goals.

"By leading to a better understanding of the root causes of crises such as migration, narcotics, disease outbreak, and food insecurity, research provides options that may help prevent the crisis from occurring, or may help stabilize the situation once it has occurred . . . Investments in strategic research are often best realized beyond an annual expenditure . . . Often ten or more years of investment in agricultural research are needed to produce new and improved crops, seeds, germ plasm, and agriculture methods. Similar long-term research investments in health and population have resulted in new diagnostic tools, new drug therapies, new contraceptives and improved family planning services . . . The impact of not doing research . . . is like slowly losing oxygen—you don't notice that it is gone until it is too late. We will not be prepared for future, unanticipated crises" (USAID Research Report 1996, 5, 12).

Since the adoption of its 1997 Strategic Plan, the Agency has also included "human capacity building through education and training" among its major goals, again acknowledging its dependency on U.S. educational institutions. As the Strategic Plan states:

> Colleges and universities produce the educated leaders and skilled professionals essential to the development of politically and economically sustainable societies, from the teachers who provide quality basic education; to the decision makers and practitioners essential to sustained growth in all sectors. Vibrant partnerships between higher education institutions, business and government are critical to a developing or transitional country's ability to solve complex problems, support a growing economy and develop sound policies. (USAID 1997, 10.)

Because of its emphasis on teaching, USAID's human-capacity goal is especially relevant to regional state colleges and even more so to the community colleges, with their expertise in technical and middle-management training.

These welcome new directions, however, can only be understood within the context of a shrinking total USAID budget. Between 1990 and 1997, U.S. official development assistance fell by more than 30 percent in constant dollars before leveling off. While no specific figures are available for higher education, the perception exists in the agency that U.S. colleges and universities may have experienced a disproportionate reduction of funds. It is also believed that the Congressional requirement for accountability reporting hits hard at long-term research and graduate education programs, since such activities seldom produce "bottom line" results fast enough for an annual report.

Official U.S. Development Assistance (in billions)

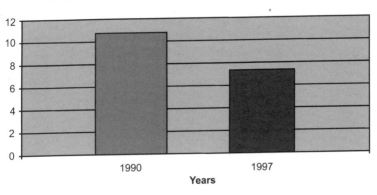

Figure 1.

Source: Official Development Assistance, Net: Source: OECD/DAC, prepared by Economic and Social Data Service (ESDS), PPC/CDIE/DI.

Other impacts of reduced funding include

- a tendency on the part of overseas USAID personnel to save money by funding in the target country or regionally rather than by funding such activities through U.S. colleges and universities; such policies do indeed get the dollars where the problem is, but tend to favor short-term, purely localized activities;

- greater use of commercial consulting firms (sometimes headed by former USAID field officers) as opposed to colleges and universities or well-established non-profit research and consulting organizations; and

- an emphasis on supporting short-term, high-volume in-country or third-country training programs rather than long-term graduate education programs for a limited number of students in the United States.

In this austere funding environment, even the number of short-term nondegree enrollments in the U.S. by overseas students is said to be down by more than half since 1995.

All these shifts and reductions in funding are understandable as part of USAID's need to cope with budgetary constraints. In some cases, the availability of resident experts and organizations in the target country may be viewed as the happy result of previous educational and development assistance efforts. But the cumulative impact of such changes is to undercut support for the international research activities of American universities and their current and future capacity to support national priorities by addressing basic development issues. In tilting the balance away from the expertise of colleges and universities over the past decade, USAID policies have also reduced the maximum help that could have been given to developing countries in educating their long-term leadership cadre—scientists, government officials, and other professionals.

United States Information Agency (USIA)

The mission of USIA "is to promote the national interest of the U.S. through understanding, informing, and influencing foreign publics and broadening dialogue between American citizens and institutions and their counterparts abroad" (USIA Program 1998, 1). Student, scholarly, and cultural exchanges are central to that mission, thus intertwining USIA activities with those of the higher education community.

Funding for all USIA programs has shrunk by 22 percent during the past five years—from $1.388 billion in 1993 to $1.077 billion in 1998 (see fig. 2). In constant dollars, that 5-year loss is almost one-third.

In October 1998, Congress mandated the consolidation of USIA into the Department of State. The consolidation is to be completed by September 30, 1999, after which USIA will cease to exist. On December 30, 1998, as required by the law, the President submitted a consolidation plan to Congress. Under the plan, USIA's Bureau of Educational and

Cultural Affairs, which administers the Fulbright Program, would be combined with the Bureau of Information, which promotes U.S. policies abroad, into a new Bureau of Information Programs and International Exchanges. However, there would be a separate congressional appropriation for exchanges. The plan could be changed before final implementation. It is too early to predict what effect, if any, the consolidation will have on appropriations for exchanges.

USIA Funding in Constant Dollars (in millions)

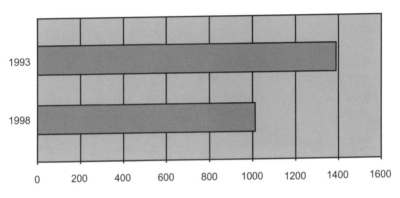

Figure 2.
Source: *U.S. Overseas Loans and Grants, July 1, 1945 September 30, 1997, USAID.*

The Fulbright Program

Fulbright is probably the best-known and most influential of all USIA exchange operations. It was established 50 years ago, in the words of its enabling legislation, to "increase mutual understanding between the people of the United States and the people of other countries." The Fulbright program has provided more than 220,000 potential leaders with the opportunity to experience and learn from others' economic and social institutions, to exchange ideas, and to embark on joint international projects that provide mutual and long-lasting benefits. Today some 4,400 Fulbright grantees from the United States and 140 other countries annually participate in the program, which includes grants for American and foreign graduating seniors and graduate students, short-term faculty exchanges, and lecturer awards.

Additional activities include teacher and administrator exchanges, institutional linkages, foreign language study, and faculty and doctoral research abroad. The list of Fulbright "alumni" includes numerous distinguished Americans and a significant leadership cadre across the globe.

> The aim of the Fulbright program is "to bring a little more knowledge, a little more reason, and a little more compassion into world affairs and thereby to increase the chance that nations will learn at last to live in peace and friendship." –Senator J. William Fulbright (Fulbright at Fifty, National Humanities Center Steering Committee on the Future of the Fulbright Educational Exchange Program, 1997).

Unfortunately, Fulbright funding has decreased dramatically since the mid-1990s. Congressional appropriations totaled $126 million in 1994, but only $99.06 million in 1996 (see fig. 3). In 1996 alone, program cuts included the loss of 130 new grants; drastic reductions in the number of grant extensions and renewals; reductions in benefits to grantees, such as tuition allowances for dependents; reduced orientation programs both for U.S. students going abroad and for foreign students coming here; cuts in the Teacher Exchange program; and elimination of regional scholar programs in the Caribbean, Latin America, and the Far East (National Humanities Center 1997, 10). Although increases in Fulbright funding have been proposed for the 1999 budget, they are slated to come at the expense of other cultural and educational programs. Only a last-minute effort in the Congress appears to have saved from the chopping block USIA's network of overseas advising centers, which served 2 million overseas students last year. These offices are the first encounter many students have with U.S. higher education and are often a critical factor in their educational decisionmaking and initial responses to this country.

It should be noted that the campuses themselves contribute substantially to Fulbright funding through cost-sharing arrangements and tuition remissions for visiting Fulbright students. The Council for the International Exchange of

Scholars (CIES) estimates that American academics serving on peer review panels and Fulbright faculty who serve as campus contacts contribute the equivalent of approximately $1 million in volunteer services.

Fulbright Funding 1994–1996 (in millions)

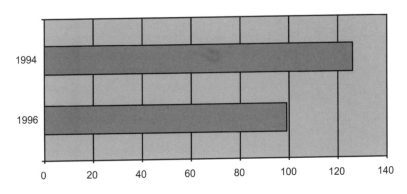

Figure 3.
Source: USIA

Recent Initiatives

While funding for traditional programs such as Fulbright has been falling, federal funds have been invested in a number of significant new initiatives that are largely oriented to the former Soviet Union and the newly independent states (NIS). The Regional Scholars Exchange Program selects scholars and university faculty in the social sciences and the humanities from all NIS countries, and Ph.D. candidates and scholars in the United States, and matches them with host institutions in the United States and the newly independent states. A similar set of Freedom Support Act Fellowships in Contemporary Issues allows government officials, nongovernmental organization (NGO) leaders, and other professionals to receive fellowships at U.S. universities and other organizations. More than a half dozen other acts, including the Edmund S. Muskie and Ron Brown fellowship programs, extend higher educational opportunities to students and scholars from the former Soviet Union and eastern and central European countries. The proliferation of such programs, when other exchange funds have fallen off, signals the change in global focus that has occurred with the ending of the Cold War.

Department of Education (DOE)

International education programs within the Department of Education are housed within two separate branches of the department. A relatively small number of grants to promote international education are made by the Fund for the Improvement of Post-Secondary Education (FIPSE) as part of its mission to assist colleges and universities in their pursuit of access and excellence. Although the majority of these grants are made to campuses interested in domestic projects, FIPSE has made awards to colleges and universities involved with internationalization activities. A recent example is the European Community/United States Joint Consortium for Cooperation in Higher Education and Vocational Education. FIPSE administers this consortium program on behalf of the United States and the European Community. This cooperative program combines student exchanges with the integration of multinational curriculums.

In 1990, Michigan State University received a three-year FIPSE grant to develop a program to work with campus and community groups to design curricular and co-curricular strategies, using the expertise brought to the campus by foreign students and U.S. students who have studied abroad. The project, initially called Strategies to Advance the Internationalization of Learning (SAIL), was based in MSU's Office of International Students and Scholars. The program, now called Raising Awareness by Internationalizing Students' Education (RAISE), is under the auspices of the Internationalizing Student Life Program. It is university-funded.

A far larger grouping of international programs resides within the Office of International Education and Graduate Programs (IEGP). Total funding for these programs is relatively small—a total of $67.5 million is appropriated for fiscal 1999—but they are influential sources of support for foreign language study and for business and international education programs. Recent funding for the business-related programs has been close to double the amount appropriated for foreign language studies. From the perspective of U.S. colleges and universities, Title VI programs are and will continue to be of the highest importance. These programs promote curricular development, support postgraduate research and exchanges, and provide invaluable assistance to area studies, foreign language, and teacher training programs.

Foreign Language and Area Study Programs

These highly influential programs, which include the Title VI Language Resource Centers and the National Resource Centers and Foreign Language and Area Studies Fellowships, are oriented toward improving the nation's capacity for foreign language and area studies. Funding under these programs is important to the nation's knowledge base in foreign language and area studies and also to its diplomatic, defense, and security goals. Although the dollar amounts involved are relatively small, such moneys are critical stimuli for institutions and their faculties and help leverage contributions from other sources. Related activities include teacher training, research, materials development, and dissemination projects in foreign language instruction and in area and international studies. Additionally, the Foreign Language and Area Studies fellowship program helps colleges and universities to provide summer and academic year awards to graduate students in foreign language, international, and area studies who seek to study abroad.

International Business Education Programs

The Business and International Education program and the Centers for International Business Education reflect the increasing tendency to link foreign language and area studies with the needs of international business and trade for such expertise. Either through direct funding or matching grants, these two programs are designed to support colleges and universities in their efforts to internationalize their business curriculums and to promote links between academic institutions and the American business community. Funding is also provided for curriculum development and research and training on issues important to U.S. trade and global competitiveness.

American Overseas Research Centers

This program offers awards to consortium of U.S. higher education institutions to establish or operate overseas centers and to promote postgraduate research, exchanges, and area studies.

Institute for International Public Policy

This institute attempts to meet the clear need to increase the representation of minorities in international service by providing grants to historically Black, Hispanic-serving, and tribally-controlled colleges and universities.

Technological Innovation and Cooperation for Foreign Information Access

This newly created program encourages collaborative use of information technologies among Title VI grant recipients, libraries, and other institutions of higher learning. Projects would collect, preserve, and provide broad access to vital materials on world regions and languages.

Under the Higher Education Act Amendments of 1998, funding for Title VI and Fulbright-Hays programs increased for the first time since 1994. The 1999 increase of 6 percent over the prior year's base restores the cost-of-living loss and actually puts Title VI in front of the inflationary curve. The turnabout in funding is partly the result of intensive efforts to forge a consensus within the higher education community on the reauthorization proposals. But it also reflects a recognition, cited in the language of the Reauthorization Act, that "the security, stability, and economic vitality of the United States in a complex global era depends upon American experts in and citizens knowledgeable about world regions, foreign languages and international affairs."

"Global competitiveness continues to drive American businessmen and their employees to sharpen their skills, enhance their productivity, and take a fresh look at their operations in view of both the challenges and opportunities presented by an international marketplace. The success of such efforts, however, relies on a thorough understanding of international diplomacy and foreign cultures . . . International education is the essential mechanism for promoting that understanding." (Higher Education Act Amendments of 1998).

Department of Defense (DOD)

In 1991, the President signed the National Security Education Act, which established the National Security Education Program (NSEP). NSEP seeks to support projects that either develop or disseminate critical information and resources that further the programmatic infrastructure of international education in the U.S. higher education community. The program underwrites projects that contribute to the national security by emphasizing the study of foreign languages, geographic regions, and fields of study deemed critical to U.S. national security. From May 1994 through May 1998, NSEP made 1,016 scholarship awards to undergraduate students and 511 fellowship awards to graduate students. Program policies and directions are provided by the Secretary of Defense in consultation with a 13-member, Presidentially-appointed board. A trust fund in the U.S. Treasury provides resources for scholarships, fellowships, and grants. NSEP obligates up to $6 million per year for awards and spends up to $8 million per year total, including program administration.

Montana State University, in cooperation with the University of Washington and six participating colleges and universities in the Northern Rockies and Great Plains, received an NSEP grant to allow students to study Basic Arabic through interactive video classes. Following two semesters of language instruction, participating students have the opportunity to study at Al Akhawayn University in Morocco.

REQUIREMENTS FOR FURTHER CHANGE

Federal funds offer institutions and faculty a wide range of opportunities for international study, travel, research, and program development. Such programs enable campuses to contribute to international understanding, stability, and economic growth and provide faculty with excellent opportunities for intellectual and personal gain. The academic relationships that such programs create among colleagues are important in creating a worldwide network of professional understanding and trust. Colleges and universities need to be fully aware of these federal resources and encourage and support faculty in seeking them. This awareness is particularly important for community and regional comprehensive colleges, which are still newcomers to the field.

At the same time, institutions must also be cognizant of changes that are working against their chances for success—significant reductions in funding, the shift to in-country or third-country education, the use of private providers, and the movement toward short-term rather than long-term goals. The major education associations have been actively representing to Congress and to the general public the problems for colleges and universities inherent in such trends and also the potential loss of quality control that may occur through the use of profit-making firms that are not subject to academic review. They argue that with their rich intellectual resources already in place, only small amounts of additional funding are needed to capitalize on existing expertise and extend it internationally. However, while maintaining their advocacy on behalf of long-term educational goals, campuses also need to adapt to change—to review their costs and to promote educational alliances with other campuses, businesses, and organizations both in this country and abroad.

SUMMARY

Neither federal nor state support appears to be adequate to the rising need for internationalization of curriculum, the expansion of student and faculty exchanges, or the support of internationally-related basic research. Long-term cutbacks in state funding for public higher education have seriously eroded the ability of public colleges and universities to reallocate resources to international education at the very time that private campuses are also facing a resource crunch. Renewal of state funding and the brightening of the financial picture for higher education generally offer an opportunity for change. Colleges and universities need to stretch their resources by developing collaborative approaches to international education. They can be significantly helped by state policies that provide incentives for internationalization of the curriculum, facilitate the enrollment of international students, and sustain study abroad programs.

The downward trend in federal funding for campus-based international programs is also taking its toll. Despite the creation of several positive new programs aimed at the former Soviet Union and eastern European states and the recent upturn in funding for Title VI, damaging impacts on higher education include

- declines in student and scholarly exchange dollars;
- replacement of long-term strategic research projects with short-term practical programs;
- substitution of short-term middle-management and technician-level training programs conducted abroad for long-term graduate education programs in the U.S.;
- greater reliance on private U.S.-based private consulting firms; and
- greater funding priority for programs linking international and business education.

Several of these trends in federal funding reinforce tendencies seen elsewhere—the preference for *in situ* programs, the shift toward business-related programs, and the general decline of funding available to higher education for international programs. These trends pose challenges to the college and university leadership as it seeks to develop funding for international education. Such trends also raise significant questions about the direction of state and federal funding and the degree to which even seemingly minor changes may be harming the ability of higher education to pursue and expand its international education mandate.

The trend among federal agencies to working directly with local higher education institutions, NGOs, and grassroots organizations in developing countries is in many ways highly desirable as part of those nations' progress toward achieving sustainable development. But the goal of indigenous self-development explains neither the assignment of educational tasks to third-party nations nor the use of commercial consulting firms for academic expertise rather than the academic institutions themselves. If there are problems with campus costs or campus accountability, they need to be reviewed and overcome. The long-standing partnership for international betterment between the federal government and the U.S. higher education community is vital to the national interest.

CHAPTER FOUR

SHIFTS IN FOUNDATION FUNDING

In 1994, U.S. philanthropic foundations awarded approximately $966 million for international activities in this country and abroad.[1] Placed against federal billions for international affairs or the trillions of dollars that flow through world markets daily, it is a modest sum but an important one. The significance of foundation funding lies not in its size but in its influence: foundations are pacesetters. As independent organizations, private philanthropic foundations have both the freedom and the wherewithal to be:

- flexible—able to respond to change rapidly;
- foresighted—able to act in advance of events;
- focused—able to concentrate their resources on a limited number of issues; and
- free—unconstrained by external political considerations (although they may have their own ideological agendas) and hence free to commit funds to controversial or politically sensitive causes.

The work of the Ford Foundation in virtually establishing the field of area studies in the post-World War II period and of the Rockefeller Foundation in pursuing developing world health issues are examples of the extraordinary impact that large-scale foundation giving can provide.

RECENT TRENDS IN INTERNATIONAL GRANTMAKING

International grantmaking in all areas, including higher education, has risen significantly since the end of the Cold War. From 1990 through 1994, giving for international purposes rose by 11.3 percent (adjusted for inflation) and has continued to rise since then. This increase was somewhat less than the increase for all grantmaking during that period.

In accordance with long-established trends, larger foundations continued to dominate the field. In 1994 more than three-quarters of all international grant dollars came from the 25 largest foundations, with the Ford Foundation alone accounting for nearly 20 percent of all spending. (This pattern is not dissimilar to foundation giving in general.) Of the 6,649 international grants conferred in 1994, the "typical" grant was only $40,000. But nearly one international dollar in five was awarded through 64 gifts, ranging from $1 million to $15 million. The top five international donor foundations in 1994 were Ford, Kellogg, MacArthur, Rockefeller, and Pew Charitable Trusts.

The geopolitical changes of the 1990s contributed to a significantly changed giving pattern during the first half of the decade. The rise of democracy, the greater openness of many nations, and the proliferation of indigenous nongovernmental organizations (NGOs) created new opportunities for grantmaking. Although funding totals were highest in sub-Saharan Africa and Latin America, the strongest growth took place in eastern Europe, where grantmaking multiplied six-fold. In-country funding grew rapidly, outpacing the funding increases for U.S.-based international organizations and programs, and much of that grantmaking was directed toward local voluntary organizations. For many foundations, giving at the grassroots level appeared the best way of getting the money to the problem, especially in regions with dire social conditions.

In the light of post-Cold War changes, international grantmaking priorities also changed. Giving increased for education, health, family planning, international development, human rights, and civil liberties. Giving decreased for exchanges, policy and research, international affairs, and peace and security studies. In the peace and security area, support shrank for national security programs and grew for international conflict and arms control. Among U.S.-based international programs, there was a steep drop in dollars for research, while funding rose for programs in primary and secondary education, adult and continuing education, community improvement, human services, primary health care, migration, refugee and civil liberties issues, media and communications, historic preservation, and the performing arts.

Giving by corporate foundations has tended to follow the expansion of their overseas business operations. Although priorities are usually set by headquarters, local managers tend to determine which local organizations to support. A 1995 report on 24 U.S. companies with major overseas involvement showed that international giving accounted for approximately 14 percent of their total contributions budget and was the most rapidly growing portion of that budget. These trends clearly reveal the influence of international trade.

Although some of the newer and smaller foundations tend to focus on domestic issues, a number have shown remarkable foresight in funding international programs. The Kunstadter Family Foundation, the Mukti Fund, and the Freeman Foundation have all given to international programs in recent years, as have grantmaking organizations such as the Global Fund for Women and the International Youth Foundations. Although international programs face stiff competition from domestic needs, community and family foundations are a promising source of future funds. Cleveland, San Francisco, and Chicago provide excellent examples of the growing role of community foundations.

Most grantmakers believe that the level of international giving will remain stable or grow in the future. Although some of the larger donors fear that the need to address domestic problems may diminish the resources available for international giving, medium and smaller donors think that interest will increase, owing to the rising interdependence of nations and the blurring of distinctions between domestic and overseas giving. A clear consensus appears among corporate funders that their international grantmaking will grow as their businesses continue to globalize. Many commentators foresee increased interest in issues such as the political participation of women, male roles in reproductive health, urban issues, sustainable resource use, and improving stability in the former Soviet Union. Other emerging issues would appear to be ethnic conflict, redefinitions of international security needs, democratization and governance, and human rights and refugee issues. Educating the general American public on international matters is also seen as a priority. This last issue clearly intersects with the mission and potential of higher education.

REQUIREMENTS FOR FURTHER CHANGE

International grantmaking in general sets the context for specific giving to international education. Many of the trends noted in the foregoing overall analysis reflect patterns already seen:

- corporate globalization;
- rising interest in eastern Europe;
- direct giving to in-country grassroots organizations rather than to U.S. domestic institutions;
- diminished interest in student, faculty, and cultural exchanges;
- emphasis on short-term, practical interventions; and
- reduced funding for scientific and policy research.

As with federal funding, almost all of these trends—although well-intentioned in themselves—move away from such fundamental educational goals as educating leaders, facilitating student and scholarly exchanges, and conducting long-term scientific and policy research. Because foundations act individually, it is not clear that there is any widespread recognition of these tendencies nor an awareness of how such trends impact the higher education community. A foundation-sponsored review or symposium on these matters may be in order.

TRENDS IN FUNDING FOR HIGHER EDUCATION

Foundation funding for international programs and activities in higher education, as a subset of all international grantmaking, totaled an estimated $165 million in 1996.[2] That is an impressive sum and represents a little over 15 percent of all foundation giving for international affairs. But it still is less than the average annual operating budget of a campus with 20,000 students, and it is only 0.15

percent of the total national annual expenditure for public higher education.

A 1998 survey by the Foundation Center, conducted specifically for this study, looked in some depth at a subset of international giving, taking into account the specific disciplines for which moneys were given. The sample included 800 large and mid-sized foundations and was limited to awards of $10,000 or more. Many of the results were startling, although some might have been anticipated from the patterns in overall international giving that have already been noted. It should also be emphasized that the survey does not include smaller foundations, such as the Stanley Foundation of Muscatine, Iowa, which has given generously to international education projects. While international giving continues strong for many of the major research institutions, other colleges and universities may need to look to local philanthropic foundations for international support, just as they are increasingly looking to local business and industry to sustain international partnerships.

Between 1990 and 1996, funding for international programs in higher education by the 800 foundations rose from $89,164,883 to $116,333,772. In constant dollars, this increase represents a real growth of 8.6 percent—roughly two-thirds the rate of increase for the overall growth rate of international grantmaking. The number of grants grew from 755 to 800 during that period, an increase of approximately 6 percent.

In both 1990 and 1996, nine academic areas accounted for more than 90 percent of all internationally related grants to higher education. Significant changes occurred in almost all of these fields, both in total giving for each area and in giving for subdisciplines within each area. Only three areas saw increased funding: higher education (but not graduate and professional education), international affairs, and the social sciences. Arts and culture, graduate and professional education, general and rehabilitative health, medical research, and science all decreased markedly. Grants to higher education for environmental protection and human rights programs also diminished, despite rising worldwide interest in these topics.

In constant dollars, many of the shifts by program area are of major magnitude (see figs. 4, 5, and 6):

Arts and Culture

Although funding for the arts in general grew during the first half of the decade, funding for higher education programs in the arts shrank between 1990 and 1996. The real dollar amount fell by 11.9 percent and the total number of grants dropped by almost a third. [3]

Higher Education

Funding for undergraduate education grew by 11.9 percent between 1990 and 1996, and the number of grants rose by almost 30 percent.

Graduate and Professional Education

The positive trend for undergraduate education was more than reversed for graduate and professional education. These areas showed a 38.8 percent funding loss and a more than 20 percent loss in the number of grants received.

Environmental Protection

Although overall interest in global environmental issues grew during this period, dollar giving for internationally-oriented environmental research, public policy, ethics, pollution control, and natural resources preservation shrank by 19.3 percent, even though the number of grants stayed constant. The dollars allocated for environmental research—small to begin with—dropped by two-thirds.

General and Rehabilitative Health

Although the number of grants remained constant, giving for general and rehabilitative health shrank by 36.8 percent. Giving for reproductive health quadrupled, but giving for public health in general fell by 91.4 percent, and the number of grants recorded in that category shrank from 19 to 12. Although it is possible that the decentralization of many public health programs among other agencies may mean that some public health expenditures are now recorded under other categories, the decline still appears to be massive.

Medical Research

Funding for medical research also fell markedly during the same time frame. Dollar awards were down by 75.6 percent, and the number of awards decreased by two-thirds. One former foundation head has noted that increases in federal National Institutes of Health (NIH) funding for medical research may have led some foundations to redirect their giving toward politically sensitive areas such as contraception and reproductive health. These reallocated dollars may be reflected in increases in other health areas. But that both overall dollars and the number of awards diminished so significantly suggests a more general trend than might be explained simply by the shift of funds from medical research to reproductive health.

International Affairs, Development, and Peace

Funding here grew by 25.5 percent, with the number of awards showing an almost 10 percent increase. However, research dollars for international affairs plummeted by 96 percent, while development and relief service dollars grew by 148.3 percent (see fig. 7). Domestic foreign policy programs—programs for foreign policy study in the U.S.—quadrupled. (This increase probably reflects the impact of about a half dozen grants of a million dollars or more, such as a $6 million grant to the University of California at Berkeley for the C. V. Starr East Asian Studies Fellowship program.) Peace, security, and arms control studies dropped 10.8 percent. Funding for college and university human rights programs fell 4.8 percent, even though overall international grantmaking in this area grew markedly during the early 1990s. Although funding for academic exchange programs rose an encouraging 23.2 percent, the number of grants in this area fell by 25 percent, suggesting larger funding but fewer recipients.

Science

Science funding plunged by an astonishing 70.4 percent over the period. The number of grants for internationally-related science programs in 1996 was 60 percent lower than it had been in 1990.

Social Science

Funding for social science soared 82 percent between 1990 and 1996, even though the number of awards stayed constant. This pattern suggests larger but not necessarily more widespread grantmaking in this area.

Increases in foundation funding for such critical areas as reproductive health and development and relief services are understandable in view of their urgency. But the accompanying steep drops in graduate education, in general and rehabilitative medicine, and in scientific and medical research are troubling. These cuts parallel trends already seen in government funding and appear to signal a widespread withdrawal of commitment to advanced study and long-term basic research within the foundation community as well as in federal agencies. The shrinkage of college and university funding even in such "hot button" areas as the environment and human rights is confusing, given the increased funding of nonacademic institutions for programs in these areas, and may suggest a lack of confidence in academia's ability to handle such problems.

U.S. Foundation Grants to Institutions of Higher Education: Nine International Program Areas: 1990–1996

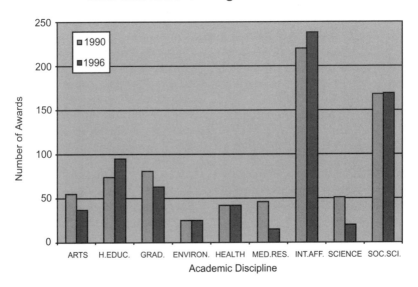

Figure 4.

U.S. Foundation Grants to Institutions of Higher Education: Nine International Program Areas: 1990–1996 (constant dollars)

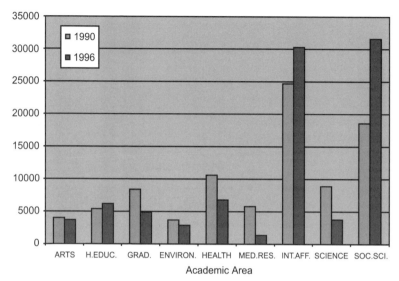

Figure 5.

U.S. Foundation Grants to Institutions of Higher Education: Nine International Program Areas: 1990–1996

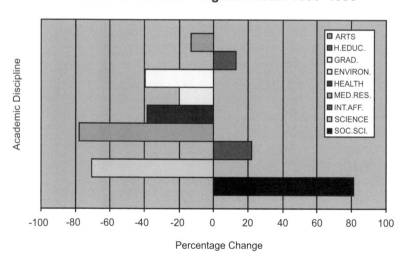

Figure 6.

U.S. Foundation Grants to Institutions of Higher Education: International Affairs Programs: 1990–1996

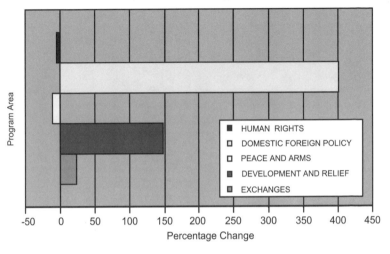

Figure 7.

REQUIREMENTS FOR FURTHER CHANGE

With only a little more than $100 million in foundation funding at stake, one cannot argue that the above-mentioned shifts in philanthropic giving will have major impacts on overall college and university operating budgets. But these trends are damaging to the higher education community, which relies on foundation funding for the "marginal" dollars that support flexibility and change. Especially now, with other funding sources stressed to the maximum, foundation support is urgently needed to encourage the transition to curriculums, research, and graduate study geared to a totally globalized society. The Ford Foundation's recent initiative to promote cross-disciplinary approaches to area studies provides an excellent example of the leadership role that philanthropic foundations can play in fostering curricular reform. Ford's venture is particularly interesting in not being limited to major research campuses but spread among a diversity of institutions.

Smaller foundations can similarly leverage change on local campuses. But, so far, the number of smaller institutions with international interests is limited.

Foundations, too, may be losing out in these shifts. They are overlooking the existing resources available to them through U.S. colleges and universities and the high standards of quality and vital reservoir of expertise these institutions represent. Part of the suggested inquiry into trends in international grantmaking should therefore include the role of higher education in international affairs and a review of those areas in which funding can be most beneficial to the sponsoring foundations, to academic institutions, and to the program or nation being helped. That dialogue should also include a candid discussion of some of the perceived weaknesses of higher education as a recipient of such awards.

FOUNDATION ATTITUDES TOWARD HIGHER EDUCATION

In their unpublished 1990 report "The Forgotten Payoff: Support for International Education Among American Private Foundations," Craufurd D. Goodwin and Michael Nacht report "mounting discouragement," among many foundation leaders, "with the capacity of higher education to serve those outside their walls and therefore to be appropriate to recipients of grants of all kinds. Not only were the social sciences frequently denounced [by foundation leaders] for self-indulgent concentration on irrelevancies but even applied sciences like agriculture were described as turning inward toward scholasticism" (Goodwin and Nacht, 1990, p. 11). American scholars, it was said, had "drifted away from reality" and tended to "talk only to themselves," (Goodwin and Nacht, 1990, p. 16) ignoring crucial societal problems. Anticipating trends recorded in the Foundation Center's 1998 study of international grantmaking, at least one foundation spokesperson "yearned for alternatives" to university-based programs and "spoke optimistically of operating exchanges in future more through non-academic non-governmental organizations than through colleges and universities."

Specifically in regard to international exchange programs, many of the foundation leaders interviewed by Goodwin and Nacht complained of:

- high tuition costs for foreign students (who, it was noted, came anyway, either on their own or funded by the United States Information Agency (USIA) or the U.S. Agency for International Development (USAID);
- the widespread perception that much faculty foreign travel did not contribute to their professional development;
- the resistance of academic institutions to having the results of their grants measured or evaluated;
- the long period of time involved in deriving any measurable benefits from exchange programs;
- isolation of exchange programs in the absence of a systemic adoption of an international perspective; and
- the irrelevance of the American experience to students' future lives in the developing world.

Informal pulse-taking among foundation leaders in 1998 finds a division of opinion on these criticisms. Some see no evidence of these criticisms among foundation decision-makers. Others believe that such fault-finding is fairly widespread. The evidence of increased overall foundation giving to college and university international programming suggests that the major donors, at least, have retained their confidence in the higher education community. But the movement toward practical, short-term projects as opposed to basic research and graduate education probably represents a combination of motives: distrust of "systems" generally, resistance to seemingly abstract scholarly endeavors, possible dissatisfaction with previous college or university experiences, and the sheer pressure of world crises that require immediate response.

SUMMARY

Private philanthropic foundations have been highly responsive to change during the 1990s. They have adapted to the rise of democracy and the development of greater indigenous grassroots leadership by moving their funding into new geographic areas and by stepping up their in-country funding to support programs that can be administered locally. The foundation community has also been highly proactive in such areas as reproductive health, urban issues, sustainable resource use, adult and continuing education, and refugee and civil liberties issues. In the multipolar post-Cold War era, marked by ethnically-based hostilities, foundations have understandably moved in the direction of conflict resolution and arms control.

In their international funding for higher education, foundations have shown an interesting and sometimes troubling pattern of support. Increases in the social sciences have been overmatched by decreases in medical and scientific research and graduate study, while the higher education community has seemingly been overlooked in funding for the rapidly growing areas of human rights and environmental protection. As we have seen, the motivations for these changes are complicated and reflect a combination of attitudes toward academe and real-world conditions that cry out for response.

Dialogue would be useful on all these topics. Higher education institutions need to look to what may be their own shortcomings and also need to recognize the direction of foundation funding flows. They should be aware of the growing potential of small, local foundations. But internationally-oriented foundations may also wish to reexamine their priorities lest, in attempting to resolve short-term problems, they fail to support the basic knowledge and high-level leadership needed for long-term change.

---

1. *All data on international grantmaking in general are taken from Loren Renz, 1997, International Grantmaking: A Report on U.S. Foundation Trends (New York, New York: The Foundation Center).*

2. *All data on grants specifically to higher education are taken from a special study conducted for this report by the Foundation Center, which analyzed grants of $10,000 or more awarded by a sample of large and mid-sized foundations to U.S.-based higher education institutions for international purposes.*

3. *All comparative figures are given in constant dollars.*

CHAPTER FIVE

NEW PLAYERS AND NEW PARTNERS

Other funding sources may be lessening, but some vibrant new alliances have resulted from the entry of new partners and new players onto the international education scene. The same forces that have driven world trade to unprecedented heights have also, by their very nature, promoted collaborations between higher education and the business sector. Academic institutions provide businesses with a ready-made, ready-to-go, cost-effective reserve of expertise, teaching skills, and technological knowledge, and their faculty and administrators often have useful contacts abroad. These "natural alliances" may involve relatively informal working arrangements between the local campus and a regional company, or they may involve large-scale and long-term relationships between a college and university (or consortium of institutions) and a major international corporation. State governments, too, are calling upon the expertise of their higher educational institutions to assist in trade and tourism activities. The broadened range of such international ventures increasingly involves regional comprehensive campuses and community colleges, as well as the more traditional international land-grant and research universities.

NEW PARTNERS: HIGHER EDUCATION AND THE BUSINESS COMMUNITY

These new partnerships between higher education and the business community take an extraordinary range of forms. Conducted in the United States, onsite in foreign countries, or through various forms of telecommunications, such programs may involve:

- tripartite collaboration (business, academia, and government) with trade missions and state and regional economic development initiatives;
- partnerships with local business and industry to offer onsite or distance education workforce training for technical and mid-management foreign workers employed in overseas business ventures;

- training programs for professionals in science, engineering, and management to help create the infrastructure needed at foreign plants and manufacturing sites;
- lifelong learning programs to help upgrade existing skills at such international locales;
- the development of on-campus international trade centers to help the local business community deal with the international marketplace;
- customized training and consulting partnerships;
- research liaisons between the university and its business partners to promote new products or technologies for foreign markets; and
- technology transfer programs in which campuses help businesses adapt cutting-edge technologies to local conditions.

Some corporations are also developing partnerships with colleges and universities that are designed to foster more general international awareness and competence among American and foreign students. Sanyo Semiconductor sponsors student interns in the United States and abroad, as does the Jaguar Corporation. With the assistance of nine corporations in the United States, Mexico, and Canada, Texas A&M University is coordinating exchanges for students in those three countries, providing them with the opportunity to study in another country (Pallan, Figueroa, Claffey, and Edelman 1995, 167). The corporations provide the money, and the university screens and selects the students. Other campuses, such as the State University of New York at New Paltz, combine short-term on-campus academic programs for foreign students with internships sponsored by American companies.

In 1997, Iowa State University received a grant from Cargill, Inc., for study abroad scholarships for students in the Colleges of Agriculture, Engineering, Business, and Liberal Arts and Sciences. There are currently over 300 ISU alumni employed at Cargill, which operates in 65 countries, with business activities in 130 more.

In many cases, universities themselves organize centers or institutes to provide a range of services for business and industry that most individual companies would find difficult and costly to establish for themselves. The Center for Technological Innovation (CIT), a cooperative venture of The California Polytechnic State University San Luis Obispo (Cal Poly) and the Technological Institute of Culiacàn (ITC) in Mexico, provides an excellent example of these new campus-industry relationships.

Created in 1993 after a series of meetings between the California Polytechnic State University and Institute of Culiacàn (ITC) faculties, the purpose of the Center for Technological Inovation includes "forming alliances among private companies, higher education institutions, and state and municipal governments; as well as the application of an industrial reactivation model that accelerates industrial development." By providing "immediate access to modern technology," the Center can help fledgling businesses reduce many of the risk factors involved in industrialization start-ups and promote job development. Positive results so far include meetings, symposiums, and short courses carried out in Culiacàn that help assess the region's human, cultural, socio-economic, and technological resources and that are developing a greater understanding about the needs of higher education institutions in the next several decades.

Programs like these offer campuses the opportunity for international connections. Some stress faculty interactions; others expand student options. Conducted outside the regular operating budget, these business-sponsored or business-related programs are, at a minimum, self-supporting and may provide some excess funds that can be allocated back to the institution as a whole—ideally, to support those international activities that are perennially short of funds.

REQUIREMENTS FOR FURTHER CHANGE

Progress is being made in establishing clearing-houses for information on existing and potential business-higher education partnerships in international activities. The University of Maryland, for example, has a database listing the programs at 75 internationally active institutions and plans to add more information and a self-updating web site. More work is needed, however, to promote data on existing operations and to provide models for successful partnerships. Individual colleges and universities need to become more aware of such opportunities and proactive in seeking them out, especially with local businesses, since such collaborations provide win-win situations that simultaneously assist regional economic development and add international opportunities for students and faculty.

Also useful would be the expansion of programs that are not necessarily linked to specific ventures, such as those sponsored by Sanyo and Jaguar, which provide internships and scholarships for students working and studying abroad. Given the difficulties of finding money for international students and new faculty positions, businesses should be encouraged to consider broader funding patterns that might include new internationally-related faculty chairs or scholarship programs. In some cases, foreign countries or companies have been known to request scholarships to the United States for their students or workers as prerequisites to a business agreement.

BUSINESS AND COMMUNITY COLLEGE PARTNERSHIPS

The pervasiveness and frequently local or regional nature of partnerships between higher education and industry are increasingly involving new kinds of institutions. While many of the comprehensive state colleges and universities have for some time been actively involved in internationally-oriented relationships with business and industry, the community colleges are the newest and perhaps most rapidly moving entrants on the scene. The strengths of the community colleges—their emphasis on lifelong learning, on vocational and technological programs, on the practical outcomes of learning, and on direct interaction with business and industry in their regions—all contribute to their rapid advancement as key players in the new global economy, with its emphasis on training and upgrade programs. Community colleges are well-attuned to working with students with limited levels of literacy and with adults returning to the job market and seeking to update their skills. Many of their programs combine learning with practicum experience. Community colleges also have the pedagogic expertise to work with middle-management and technical employees who need further on-the-job training. The following brief examples give some flavor of the range of community colleges' participation in international education programs.

Microenterprise and Small Business Development
Sinclair Community College, the Eastern Iowa Community College District, and 60 other member campuses in Community Colleges for International Development have trained more than 600 students from Madras, India, in tailoring, geriatric home health care, engine repair, small business development, and total quality management. The training is conducted in collaboration with Indian educators, voluntary agency personnel, and local crafts- and businesspersons.

Trade Assistance Partnerships
The Business and Industry Center at Edison Community College in Piqua, Ohio, trains and informs manufacturers on the export potential of such regional products as textiles, electronics equipment, consumer appliances, and heavy and light machinery.

Teaching Technical English
Delaware Community College, near Philadelphia, offers English language training to administrators and science faculty at the Czech Technical University in Prague and, with other community colleges, to institutions in Estonia, Latvia, Lithuania, and Slovakia.

Training Trainers
El Paso Community College is strengthening the credentials of elementary school teachers in El Salvador, many of whom have not completed their high school education.

Databases and Information Networks
The American Council on International Intercultural Education, a subsidiary program of the American Association of Community Colleges, is cataloguing the international and intercultural expertise of its member colleges to help identify institutions having experience with specific activities in different regions of the world.

Telecommunications and Distance Learning
Three California community colleges—Cerritos Community College, Santa Barbara City College, and the Coast Community Colleges—are cooperating with Ural State University in Russia in order to develop effective telecourse techniques and to assess delivery mechanisms. California community colleges have also assisted with alternative learning modalities in Argentina, Chile, Japan, and Mexico.

REQUIREMENTS FOR FURTHER CHANGE

The positive direction already taken by other higher education institutions and now being taken by the community colleges needs to persist and expand. Local chambers of commerce and other regional economic development organizations must continue to be attuned to these possibilities. Businesses should be encouraged to realize the many ways in which colleges and universities contribute to the attractiveness of their communities as sites for international trade.

As with other colleges and universities, the internationalization of community colleges should also begin to penetrate the curriculum more directly. Significant numbers of community colleges cite financial and staffing difficulties as barriers to the expansion of their international education programs. Recruiting international students, especially in the absence of residential facilities on campus, is also a problem. If these campuses are to become more international, they need to move study abroad, recruitment of foreign students, and internationalization of the curriculum higher on their priority list. Collaboration between community colleges, regional comprehensive campuses, and nearby land-grant universities could help resolve some of these problems by allowing for shared faculty expertise, shared recruitment efforts, and even shared housing opportunities for international students. International coursework could also be fostered through collaborative use of telecommunications.

PARTNERSHIPS WITH THE STATES

In the new internationalized economic order, the states, too, are systematically forming new and significant partnerships with their colleges and universities. North Carolina, for example, has expanded its international education programs to enhance cultural awareness and make the state more attractive to foreign business and investments. The state aims at creating a seamless educational program, from kindergarten through college, that will build greater global understanding and help reinforce the high priority North Carolina gives to foreign trade and tourism (Governor's 1998, n.p.).

A number of other states have also been proactive in including colleges and universities in their trade missions and encouraging and supporting international activities on campus as part of their own economic development programs. The International Business Development Center of Michigan State University, for example, is a longtime national leader in export development training. But such activities are far from their potential. Although state international budgets rose dramatically between 1984 and 1990, the early 1990s saw a decline in such ventures. A 1995 study shows most state trade assistance services focusing on a single activity—training exporters' staffs to handle export operations—and, even here, reaching only a very limited number of firms (Conway and Northdurft 1996, 11).

REQUIREMENTS FOR FURTHER CHANGE

States could make a major contribution to creating an international outlook among their citizenry by looking at their K–12 curriculums, with particular attention to foreign language instruction. Performance awards or other strategies to encourage innovation might also be used to stimulate and reward internationalization of the curriculum at the college level. About 15 states have been experiencing shrinking foreign student enrollments (Davis 1998, 31–32); a review of recruitment and retention strategies, especially tuition policies, needs to be undertaken.

States are also not making full use of the international expertise available to assist their foreign trade ventures. More extensive use of the resources available through existing faculty and programs on their campuses would benefit both the states and their academic institutions.

SUMMARY

Directly and indirectly, the new partnerships with business and with state governments contribute to the internationalization of the campus. Faculty and students move more readily across borders and continents; campus awareness of global affairs is heightened; students become more familiar with the international nature of the job market; and motivation increases to strengthen the international elements in the curriculum. The expansion of international activities into the community colleges adds another 10.6 million students to the number of undergraduates who can benefit from international exposure. The new partnerships provide an exciting leaven for higher education that broadens its perspective and adds new resources.

But collaboration with the business community is not a panacea for all international education problems. Partnerships between business and higher education, however valuable in themselves, do not support curriculum, provide only limited support for exchange programs, and are not directed to long-term research projects that may or may not be ultimately profitable. All of these activities need not only seed money but also sustained support that is willing to wait for results. New pharmaceuticals, for example, that might alleviate diseases endemic to a developing region but that are not prevalent in the United States are not cost-effective investments for industry, necessary though they may be to regional and world health. The same caveats can be also offered in regard to collaborations between campuses and their state governments.

In looking to the future, it is important to remember that international education is about ideas and ideals as well economic development. It requires:

- a curriculum with a global perspective that describes and explains both the commonalities and differences of diverse cultures and histories;
- a recognition that one of the best ways to achieve such understandings is through the exchange of students and scholars;

- a sense of "social stewardship" that recognizes the interdependency of people and countries and the responsibility of countries such as the United States for promoting worldwide health, environmental conditions, human potential, and social stability (Mazur and Sechler 1997, 6); and

- a commitment to basic knowledge and research into the scientific and social issues that underlie the uneven economic development of nations.

To achieve such goals, higher education needs its own resolve—the support of trustees, administrators, and faculty for these aims. Business and government can help, but the fundamental decisions depend upon the campus, its leadership, its willingness to make international education an institutional imperative, and the availability of adequate resources to implement its goals.

CHAPTER SIX

OUTLOOK FOR INTERNATIONAL EDUCATION

Paying for international education has traditionally involved a complex partnership. In the past, partners have included campuses, students, state and federal governments, and private philanthropy. Today, business and industry have become important players, too. Schematized as simply as possible, the roles of each of these partners reveal a dynamically interrelated network of support for internationally-related instruction, exchanges, and research.

The campuses. Most of the money for international programs comes from campus operating budgets. Those dollars fund the faculty and facilities needed for international programs. This support can be clearly seen in the monies provided for such explicitly international programs as foreign language or area studies. But operating support also sustains faculty, equipment, and laboratories in disciplines, such as biology, that can be applied to international research activities. Faculty exchanges and support services for foreign students also depend on operating budgets.

The students. Foreign students in the United States and U.S. students abroad support their own overseas education through tuition payments or, to a very limited degree, through scholarship assistance.

State governments. State tax revenues foot most of the bill for the operating costs of public colleges and universities. State dollars partially subsidize tuition costs for domestic students and, to a diminishing degree, for foreign students, whose tuition payments at public colleges and universities do not always cover the costs of their education.

The federal government. Federal programs have traditionally leveraged the existing academic resources of colleges and universities to support government research priorities and academic and cultural exchange programs. Federal funding has also traditionally been used to support specially designated programs in such strategic areas as foreign language and area studies.

Private philanthropy. Private philanthropic dollars have in the past gone to a wide range of internationally-related activities: education, art and culture, public health, medicine, the environment, international affairs, and the social sciences. Foundation-sponsored programs in these fields have included curricular development; student, faculty, and cultural exchanges; and basic and applied research.

Business community. Although corporate foundations have customarily reserved some funds for overseas expenditure, the business community has only recently been a major player in funding international education.

Unfortunately for international education, all but the last of these traditional funding areas are either shifting focus or diminishing.

Campus budgets. Public and private college and university operating budgets have been stretched for almost a generation now. The ability to replace faculty, especially in low-enrollment fields such as foreign languages, has shrunk markedly, leaving many gaps in coverage. Many would argue that prolonged funding shortages have encouraged a stand-pat mentality among faculty and an unwillingness to engage in curricular innovation.

Student tuition costs. Tuitions have risen dramatically at public and private universities. With most foreign students paying their own way, the sharply increased cost of a U.S. education has probably contributed to the recent slow growth of such enrollments.

State support. Falling state support is at the root of public campus difficulty in meeting operating costs. The rise in tuition between 1980 and 1996 exactly matched the loss of state operating dollars. Some state support exists for campus-sponsored foreign-trade activities, but such funding has been limited so far.

Federal support. Federal dollars have been falling for foreign affairs and foreign assistance generally. The new emphasis on building human resource capacity and on funds for eastern Europe and the former Soviet Union provide new opportunities for campuses, including state and community colleges, to engage in overseas activities, often in formerly closed areas of the world. But the persistent fall-off in support for basic research and graduate study and for such staples as the Fulbright program threatens long-term harm to America's ability to address root problems in health, agriculture, and the environment, or to help build a democratically inclined leadership cadre in developing countries. The modest increase in Title VI funding for fiscal 1999 may presage a hopeful reversal of these trends.

Philanthropic support. Many of the trends in federal funding are reflected in patterns of private foundation support for international education. The total dollars involved have risen slightly in the past five years, but the focus has shifted toward grassroots, short-term, in-country assistance designed to resolve a specific problem or meet a short-term need rather than toward basic research or high-level leadership training. The cuts—many of them massive—in foundation support for U.S. campus-based graduate education, public health programs, medical research, science, and environmental programs appear to be harbingers of a profound pragmatism that will not fund programs that do not promise clear, short-term, and unambiguous results.

Business community. Unlike the other funding partners, the business community has been increasing its engagement with international education programs on campus. Overseas giving by corporate foundations has increased, but far more important for American colleges and universities have been their growing partnerships with the business community. Not only traditional research universities but state and community colleges as well are being tapped to assist businesses with trade missions, with in situ or distance-learning overseas training programs, and with targeted programs of applied research. Some firms have sponsored student internships or exchange programs as part of their overall

goodwill gestures. But for the most part, the programs
have been short-term and practical and have involved
applied rather than basic research and mid-management
or technical training rather than graduate or advanced
study. This bottom-line orientation has enabled many
campuses to engage in exciting and useful overseas
projects, but it has not paid the bill for more
fundamental expenditures.

OUTLOOK FOR INTERNATIONAL EDUCATION

A similar contrast between dynamism and diminishing
energies can also been seen in international education
itself. Some of the boldest and most venturesome new
developments are being driven by the interactions between
academe and the external world of business and technology.
Thanks to telecommunications, the melting boundaries of
space and time enable any campus and any faculty member
to pursue "virtual" educational contact anyplace on earth,
usually at far less cost than the cost of establishing such
programs physically at a nearby off-campus site. Electronic
contacts and partnerships among faculty with similar
academic interests have similarly proliferated. On the other
hand, a review of curricular change shows many programs
still "dug in," with outmoded approaches to international
studies and a drop in actual as opposed to virtual
international travel and study by faculty.

The general pattern for the academic aspects of international
education might thus be seen as a melange of movement and
stasis, with the most energetic and innovative approaches
seen in business schools and in the applications of
technology, but with stasis or even stagnation in more
traditional areas. As we have seen, plummeting foreign
language enrollments, rigidities in area studies and
international relations curriculums, and slow-growth foreign
student enrollments are all symptoms of inadequacies within
the total picture for international education.

International education is not in crisis, but neither its
programs nor its funding is commensurate with the needs of
a global society. The goals of international education are to

educate generalists, train specialists, foster human and cultural exchanges, and support research directed toward fundamental global problems. Our response is clearly inadequate in all these areas:

- American college graduates are all-too-likely to enter a global society without knowledge of a single foreign language or culture and without the general knowledge that prepares them for global citizenship. They are far less prepared than young people from other countries to compete for global commerce or market share.

- Our international affairs specialists, many believe, are not being given the interdisciplinary or problem-oriented skills they need for today's and tomorrow's complex world. Cutbacks in funding for graduate study, research, and exchanges also mean that many of them have not had the essential in-depth experience of living in a foreign country and absorbing its culture. Graduate study in general—both for U.S. citizens studying abroad and for gifted foreign nationals coming here for doctoral work—is being eroded by the priority given to short-term programs.

- Internationally-oriented research programs are especially problematic at this time. Leveraged through existing campus resources, basic research programs are deeply dependent on external sponsorship, primarily through the federal government, although foundation funding in health, medicine, and agriculture has also been an important component of assistance. The increasing emphasis by both the federal government and the philanthropic community on short-term applied research programs means that many fundamental global issues— and global threats—are being ignored. The long-term impact of such shortsightedness may well be severe.

International education, by its very nature, is driven by change. But it is the most vocal and visible elements of change that dominate the response. The growing force of international commerce and communications, the ever-expanding power of technology, and the urgency of world crisis situations are increasingly shaping curriculums, exchanges, and research. In so fluid a situation, what might be called the infrastructure of international education—its traditional academic programs and its emphasis on graduate study and research—tend to disappear.

Long experience has made both academic and political leaders as well as philanthropists suspicious of systems or five-year plans. Nevertheless, it has been a combination of state and federal funding and philanthropic dollars that has spearheaded and initiated academic change in the past, whether through Title VI, the Fulbright program, or the powerful influence of major foundations such as Ford or Carnegie. Today, with additional players such as multinational companies and small and regional foundations on the scene, guiding change for international education is an even more complex and delicate task. Without attempting to be prescriptive, the following policy recommendations suggest some actions that academic institutions, state and federal governments, and the philanthropic and business communities might take to sustain the existing vibrancy of international education programs and to redirect energy to static or neglected areas.

POLICY RECOMMENDATIONS

The advent of the year 2000 marks an appropriate anniversary for reviewing the importance of international education to this country's intellectual resources and to its strategic priorities. For each of the partners in international education, the advent of the new millennium poses both the necessity and a symbolic occasion for constructive renewal and growth. More money alone is not the answer to many of the issues cited above; money is valuable only as a support for clearly defined program needs. Although the cutbacks have certainly taken their toll, what is needed—and what this list of policy recommendations attempts to detail—is a combination of commitment to and adequate support for the goals of international education, together with clear focus, good management, and accountable use of resources.

Academic world. Academic institutions do not, by and large, coordinate their activities with one another. Each campus, under state or trustee guidance, develops and pursues its mission and sets its own funding priorities.

It is therefore recommended that each campus:

- review and, if necessary, revise its mission and curriculum to include an emphasis on international education, both in the general education curriculum and in the disciplines;
- specifically review the status of foreign language instruction, area studies, and international relations on campus;
- recognize the importance of international study and travel for faculty development;
- pursue both the enrollment of overseas students and study abroad programs and provide needed support programs for both groups of students;
- look to its potential role in development assistance and other overseas education or research programs;
- give high priority to international education programs in its resource allocation process;
- promote collaborative efforts with other academic institutions and intra-institutional efforts with business or teacher education programs to maximize and share resources;
- seek to diversify its funding through philanthropic and business support; and
- improve accountability in order to address existing criticisms of higher education, especially in the philanthropic community.

The national higher education associations also have a role to play in promoting international education within the campus community and advocating its importance with state and federal funding agencies.

State governments. State governments have the opportunity to use the current improved financial climate to restore some of the funding that has been lost to public institutions—and to private institutions, too, in many cases. Such restoration of the operating budget is imperative to provide the basic operating resources needed to hire new faculty, maintain facilities, and provide needed upgrades in laboratories, libraries, and information technology. Beyond this "bread-and-butter" support, states can assist in the development of international education "literacy" by:

- targeted funding for specific areas, such as foreign language instruction or area studies;
- tuition policies that encourage international student enrollment;
- specific targets to increase the number of students in study-abroad programs; and
- expanded use of existing academic expertise and resources in promoting international trade opportunities by working with state and regional economic development offices.

Federal government. Federal government policies in regard to support of international education programs here in the United States are part of a much larger pattern of diminishing international affairs funding. Federal policies are also increasingly governed by Congressional demands for accountability, which promote an emphasis on large numbers and short-term results. The consolidation of federal agencies dealing with exchange programs may encourage more broad-based policy considerations in that area. But it would probably be very useful for colleges and universities, through their national higher educational organizations, to mount a forceful advocacy campaign that would argue the importance of basic research, graduate study, and exchange programs. Such a public policy campaign should also focus on the enormous resource—financial and otherwise—provided by foreign students in the United States and the importance of overseas advising offices as their first contact with America.

Philanthropic community. As in the academic world, much of the strength of the foundation community lies in its intellectual independence. Foundations tend to pursue their own goals, with only moderate regard for the priorities of other philanthropic organizations. Nevertheless, the foundation community as a whole has clearly moved over the past five years to replace some of its badly needed traditional support for advanced study and basic research with more short-term and applied projects. As previously noted, there are many reasons for these changes: the urgent needs of developing countries, the emergence of local leadership and expertise, the proportion of federal funding that may be available in these areas. But support for higher education and support for international projects are far from mutually exclusive. Indeed, the international research capability of American campuses and their ability to help educate future foreign experts and leaders are essential elements in promoting international peace and prosperity. Especially in view of the similar tendencies toward short-term objectives reflected in federal funding priorities, it is important that:

• foundations review their own international education priorities in the light of developing trends throughout the foundation community;

• they especially review the reductions in funding to American colleges and universities for public health, medical and scientific research, environmental studies, and graduate education; and

• they facilitate such review by convening a conference or symposium on international education priorities among major foundation leaders.

Business community. In a knowledge society, business and academe increasingly interact. Such interactions now encompass both international training programs and research. Colleges and universities need actively to seek out such partnership opportunities, recognizing the mutual benefits they confer. Both groups need to appreciate their interdependence and the attractions that local campuses hold for foreign businesses. For the campuses themselves, it is important that they:

• continue to document and publicize existing programs and areas of expertise, as is being done by the University of Maryland electronic database; and

• whenever possible, encourage their business partners to sponsor student and faculty exchanges or support faculty positions as ancillaries to their more short-term goals.

Many overseas companies in the developing world or in nations such as China are eager to give their own employees the possibility of study in the United States. Such scholarship programs are options worth pursuing.

SUMMARY

International education is in flux. Time-honored approaches are waning in some cases, but the horizon is bright with exciting new opportunities. New programs, new institutions, and new partners are the inevitable corollaries of a world as "wired" as ours by interwoven networks of trade and communications and, unfortunately, also by the collective dangers posed by global economic inequality, disastrous environmental and climatic shifts, and the ever-expanding threat of ethnic conflict.

As the new millennium begins, international education is at once more important and less secure than in the recent past. The very nature of our global society carries with it the inescapable necessity for adaptation to change, but the higher education community is not moving as rapidly or as effectively as it should to respond to new curricular imperatives. Nor is there a clear national consensus on the need for expanded student and scholarly exchanges or for the graduate study and basic research that provide future leadership and assist in long-term problem resolution.

The academic community must strengthen its own resolve to place international education high on its list of priorities. But our colleges and universities can only succeed as part of a national partnership that recognizes the importance of preparing college graduates for a globalized future and of sustaining the reservoir of scholarly expertise that underpins both basic and applied research. Both global stewardship and national self interest demand a renewal of commitment to the curricular fundamentals that underpin all aspects of international education, to the humanistic as well as the practical aspects of faculty and student exchanges, and to the basic research that alone will build for a better tomorrow. Higher education, state and federal governments, and the philanthropic community all need to underscore the importance of being intellectually and culturally prepared to live on an ever-shrinking globe and to find both the will and the resources to promote such change.

REFERENCES

Altbach, Philip G., and Lionel S. Lewis. 1997. Internationalism and Insularity: American Faculty and the World. In Open Doors: 1996–1997 Report on International Educational Exchange. Edited by Todd M. Davis. New York: Institute of International Education.

American Association of State Colleges and Universities (AASCU). 1998. Higher Education Development Linkages: Sample Profiles at the State Colleges and Universities. Washington, D.C.

American Council on Education (ACE). 1998. Educating for Global Competence. Washington, D.C.: American Council on Education.

"Boise State University in Vietnam Develop M.B.A. Program." April 28, 1995. The Chronicle of Higher Education, A44 (http://chronicle.com).

Building the Global Community: The Next Step. 1994. Report of a conference sponsored by the American Council on International Intercultural Education and the Stanley Foundation, Warrenton, VA, November 28–30, 1994.

Cage, Mary Crystal. October 18, 1996. "Enrollment in Spanish Courses Increases to Record Level." The Chronicle of Higher Education, A12 (http://chronicle.com).

Cage, Mary Crystal. August 18, 1995. "Mary Baldwin College Starts New Program in Foreign Studies." Chronicle of Higher Education, A16 (http://chronicle.com).

Chandler, Alice. 1998. Public Higher Education and the Public Good: Public Policy at the Crossroads. Washington, D.C.: American Association of State Colleges and Universities.

College of Agriculture. 1997 Annual Report. Ames, Iowa: Iowa State University.

"Consortium Seeks Links with Brazil, Indonesia, Turkey." April 28, 1995. Chronicle of Higher Education, A67 (http://chronicle.com).

Conway, Carol, and William E. Northdurft. 1996. The International State: Crafting a Statewide Trade Development System. Washington, D.C.: The Aspen Institute Rural Economic Policy Program.

Davis, Todd M., ed. 1997. Open Doors: 1996–1997 Report on International Educational Exchange. New York: Institute of International Education.

Davis, Todd M., ed. 1998. Open Doors: 1977–1998 Report on International Educational Exchange. New York: Institute of International Education.

Educating for Global Competence. Washington, DC: American Council on Education.

Engerman, David C. and Masden, Parker G. 1992. In the International Interest: The Contributions and Needs of America's International Liberal Arts Colleges. Beloit, WI: International Liberal Arts Colleges.

Fulbright at Fifty, National Humanities Center Steering Committee on the Future of the Fulbright Educational Program, July 1997.

Goodman, Allan E. November 8, 1996. "College Courses Must Take a New Approach to Foreign Affairs." Chronicle of Higher Education, A52 (http://chronicle.com).

Goodman, Louis W., Kay King, and Nancy L. Ruther. 1994. Undergraduate International Studies on the Eve of the Twenty-first Century. Washington, D.C.: Association of Professional Schools of International Affairs.

Goodwin, Craufurd D., and Michael Nacht. 1990. The Forgotten Payoff: Support for International Education Among American Private Foundations: A Report to the American Council of Learned Societies and the John D. and Catherine T. MacArthur Foundations.

Governor's Global Forum III. 1998. Greensboro, N.C.

Haakenson, Paul. 1994. Recent Trends in Global/International Education, ERIC Digest, ED373021: 1.

Hanson, Katherine H., and Joel W. Meyerson, eds. 1995. International Challenges to American Colleges and Universities: Looking Ahead. Washington, D.C.: American Council on Education/Oryx Press.

Hill, Christopher. 1994. Academic International Relations: The Siren Song of Policy Relevance. In Two Worlds of International Relations: Academics, Practitioners and the Trade in Ideas, edited by Christopher Hill and Pamela Beshoff. London: Routledge.

Lebow, Richard Ned. January 2, 1996. "Cold War Lessons for Political Theorists." Chronicle of Higher Education, B1 (http://chronicle.com).

Magner, Denise K. March 9, 1994. "Oregon State Adds International Flavor to Students' Majors." Chronicle of Higher Education, A19 (http://chronicle.com).

Mazur, Laurie Ann, and Susan E. Sechler. 1997. Global Interdependence and the Need for Social Stewardship. Paper No. 1, Global Interdependence Initiatives, Rockefeller Brothers Fund. New York, New York: Rockefeller Brothers Fund.

Monaghan, Peter. May 30, 1990. "Boyer: American Education Fails in World Understanding," The Chronicle of Higher Education, A30 (http://chronicle.com).

"New Law Makes Foreign Students, Scholars Feel Unwelcome." November 29, 1996. Chronicle of Higher Education, A45.

Official Development Assistance, Net: Source: OECD/DAC, prepared by Economic and Social Data Service (ESDS), PPC/CDIE/DI. OECD: Washington, DC.

Pallan Figueroa, Carlos, Joan M. Claffey, and Alan Edelman, eds. 1995. The Relevance of Higher Education to Development. Asociación Nacional de Universidades e Instituciones de Educación Superior, Association Liaison Office for University Cooperation in Development, Institute of International Education.

Partnerships for Global Development: The Clearing Horizon: A Report of the Carnegie Commission on Science, Technology and Government. 1992.

Pesek, Robert. 1997. The Role of ESL Instruction in the U.S. Economy. In Open Doors: 1996–1997 Report on International Educational Exchange. Edited by Todd M. Davis. New York: Institute of International Education.

Pickert, Sarah M. 1992. "Preparing for Global Community: Achieving an International Perspective in Higher Education." ERIC Higher Education Reports, 92-2. Washington, D.C.: Association for the Study of Higher Education/ERIC Clearinghouse on Higher Education.

Pinstrup-Anderson, Per, Matthias Lundberg, and James L. Garrett. 1995. Foreign Assistance to Agriculture: A Win-Win Proposition. Food Policy Report. Washington, D.C.: The International Food Policy Research Institute.

Renz, Loren. 1997. International Grantmaking: A Report on U. S. Foundation Trends. New York, New York: Foundation Center.

"Researchers Say Study Abroad is Key to Learning Languages." February 7, 1997. Chronicle of Higher Education, A45 (http://chronicle.com).

Rossman, Parker. 1992. The Emerging Worldwide Electronic University: Information Age Global Higher Education. Contributions to the Study of Education, no. 57. Westport, Conn.: Greenwood Press.

"Unemployment Rate for Ph.D.'s Hit 10-Year High." January 12, 1996. Chronicle of Higher Education, A15. (http://chronicle.com).

U.S. Agency for International Development (USAID). 1998. 1997 Agency Performance Report. Washington D.C.: Center for Development Information and Evaluation.

U.S. Agency for International Development (USAID). 1997. Strategic Plan. Washington, DC: USAID.

USAID Research Report, April 15, 1996, 11. Washington, DC: USAID.

U.S. Information Agency (USIA). Date. Program and Budget in Brief, Fiscal Year 1998. Washington, DC: USAID.

Voght, Geoffrey M., and Ray Schaub. 1992. Foreign Languages and International Business, ERIC Digest, ERIC ED347851 (September 1992) : 1,3.

Volkman, Toby A. "Crossing Borders," Ford Foundation Report (Winter 1998): 28–29. New York, New York: The Ford Foundation.

Watkins, Beverly T. February 20, 1991. "Project Delivers Foreign Newspapers Via Computer." Chronicle of Higher Education, A23 (http://chronicle.com).

Wilson, David L. September 16, 1992. "Electronic Comic Books Aid Language Study at Stanford." Chronicle of Higher Education, A24 (http://chronicle.com).